The Poetics of Ascent

SUNY Series in Judaica: Hermeneutics, Mysticism, and Culture

Michael Fishbane, Robert Goldenberg, and
Arthur Green, Editors

The Poetics of Ascent

THEORIES OF LANGUAGE
IN A RABBINIC ASCENT TEXT

Naomi Janowitz

STATE UNIVERSITY OF NEW YORK PRESS

Published by
State University of New York Press, Albany

© 1989 State University of New York

Printed in the United States of America

For information, address State University of New York
Press, State University Plaza, Albany, N.Y., 12246

Library of Congress Cataloging in Publication Data
Janowitz, Naomi.
The poetics of ascent.
(SUNY series in Judaica)
Bibliography: p.
Includes index.
    1. Merkava. 2. Ascension of the soul – History of
doctrines. I. Title. II. Series.
BM635.J36 1988 296.7′1 87-9993
ISBN 0-88706-636-4
ISBN 0-88706-637-2 (pbk.)

For my parents

Contents

Contents

Preface

The rabbinic ascent text which is the focus of this study, *Maaseh Merkabah* (The Working of the Chariot), was first edited by Gershom Scholem in 1965. Despite numerous studies of this and other Hekhalot (palace) mystical texts, debate has centered largely on Scholem's original agenda, that is, the dating of the texts to the first century (i.e., pre-Christian) and their status in relation to "normative" Judaism. This study takes a different tack: it attempts to analyze this lush, often cryptic text using methods for studying ritual language developed by anthropologists and linguists. These methods are predicated on a notion of the multifunctionality of language. Explanations of the continuing power of ritual language must go beyond attention to propositional information and attempt to locate the basis for this power in culturally specific ideologies of language. Some of the best evidence for reconstructing ideologies of language is found in the structures and forms of ritual texts themselves. Using these methods with a rabbinic ascent text is not an easy task, faced with an often puzzling Hebrew text which is impossible to date precisely on the one hand, and with competing strategies for studying ritual language, often articulated in highly specialized vocabularies, on the other hand.

Chapter One attempts to survey modern scholarship both on *Maaseh Merkabah* and on current theories of ritual language. It discusses the need for, and the appropriateness of, the matching of text and methods. Chapter Two reviews the problems in dating and locating the text, and then raises the tricky question of "rabbinic" ideologies of language by surveying a variety of texts for ideas about the function of the divine name. The last section of the chapter turns to the text itself and focuses on the ideology of the divine name and divine language. Chapter Three contains the translation as well as variants from other sources. Chapter Four relates the forms of the text (repetitive, hymnic formulas embedded within reported speech) to the emerging ideology of language. Recitation of the text as a whole is efficacious because the verses contain divine speech and the name of the deity that cannot be merely "mentioned" or quoted without engaging the power inherent in the divine name. Finally, in Chapter Five the conclusions from studying *Maaseh Merkabah* are used to reflect on the general debate about ritual language. How do ritual texts work? How are they creative? The main concern is the multifunctionality of language and the interactions between these functions.

Acknowledgments

I would like to thank Michael Silverstein, Richard Parmentier, Moshe Idel, Kathleen Shelton, and David Blumenthal. In addition, I would like to thank the Fulbright Foundation, the Dorot Foundation and the University of California at Davis, Office of Research, for their support. Mary Doty helped in the preparation of the manuscript. The late David Wilmot helped with the Hebrew translation.

Abbreviations

b. = Babylonian Talmud

t. = Tosefta

j. = Jerusalem Talmud

Tractates of Mishnah, Tosefta and Talmud

A.Z.	Azodah Zara
Ber.	Berakot
Er.	Erubin
Hag.	Hagigah
Kid.	Kidushin
Meg.	Megillah
Men.	Menahot
Ned.	Nedarim
Pes.	Pesahim
R.H.	Rosh Hashana
Sanh.	Sanhedrin
Sot.	Sotah
Yoma	Yoma
Zeb.	Zebahim

Midrash

Mek.	Mekilta de-Rabbi Ishmael, ed. J. Lauterbach (Philadelphia, 1949)
Abd. R. Natan	Abot d'Rabi Natan
Eccl. R.	Ecclesiastes Rabba
Ex. R.	Exodus Rabba
Num. R.	Numbers Rabba
Pesik R.	Pesikta Rabbati
PRE	Pesikta Rabbi Eleazer

Transliteration Chart

א	= '		מ ם	= M
ב	= B		נ ן	= N
ג	= G		ס	= S
ד	= D		ע	= '
ה	= H		פ ף	= P
ו	= W		צ ץ	= Ṣ
ז	= Z		ק	= Q
ח	= Ḥ		ר	= R
ט	= Ṭ		שׁ	= Š
י	= Y		שׂ	= Ś
כ ך	= K		ת	= T
ל	= L			

CHAPTER ONE

Images of Ascent

Rabbi Ishmael said: I asked of Rabbi Akiba a prayer that a man does when ascending to the chariot . . . he said "Purity and holiness are in his heart and he prays a prayer." (Lines 5-10)

Rabbi Akiba said: . . . In the first palace stand 4,000 myriads of chariots of fire and 2,000 myriads of flames are interspersed between them. (Lines 198, 204-206).

The fiery descriptions of the heavens presented by Rabbi Akiba introduces his student Rabbi Ishmael to the world of ascent, trips through the heavens for the purpose of seeing the upper realm and all its inhabitants. This portrayal of the process of ascent – and the vision achieved – are from one of the loosely defined group of Hekhalot (palace) or Merkabah (chariot) texts. These texts confuse the reader with their lush, repetitive, and at times nonsensical language, and confound scholars with their diverse, hard-to-decipher manuscript evidence. What are these cryptic, sometimes mystical, sometimes magical texts about? This study is an attempt to select one manuscript version of one Hekhalot text and, by studying its content and literary forms, gain insight into what ascent is perceived to entail and why the characters are so concerned with understanding and teaching each other about ascent and visions of the heavenly realm.

The literary motif of ascent in Late Antique religious texts has received widespread attention.[1] Since the work of Gershom Scholem, debate has also focused on the possible Late Antique date of Hebrew texts in which ascent motifs appear to describe ascent as a ritual practice.[2] He believed that as early as the pre-Christian era, Jews not only told stories about ascent but themselves attempted to attain heavenly visions. One text that seems to represent the image of ascent as an obtainable ritual object was cited at the start of the chapter, *Maaseh Merkabah* (The Working of the Chariot),[3] characterized by one scholar as part of a collection of "technical guides or manuals for mystics."[4] The form of the text is a

1

continuous set of dialogues in which Rabbi Ishmael questions the cele-
brated mystical figures Rabbi Akiva and Rabbi Nehunya, as well as
assorted angelic figures, about the process of ascent. As often as not, they
reply to him in hymns descriptive of the heavens the mystic is traversing
but that, since the hymns are indeed answers, at the same time seem to
have the weight of instructions to an aspirant. It is as though Rabbi Ishmael would himself ascend if he could perfectly understand the wordings
and implications of these hymns. Importantly, in *Maaseh Merkabah* the
reader is never directly informed where these dialogues, so other-worldly
in their content, are taking place. Throughout the text, Ishmael's role is
preponderantly that of a questioner, but at least once, having received the
"announcement" of a description of heaven from Nehunya, he seems
himself to look directly at all the palaces of heaven; that is, to ascend.

It is in particular the exact words spoken by each mystical figure in
his ascent that most interests Ishmael, as though he senses that the words
themselves empower the ascender. His very first question in the text, to
Rabbi Akiba, is about the "prayer that a man does when ascending to the
chariot," as though the prayer itself were a deed. What is more, each
character he addresses offers him examples of language that "does"; that
is, words that effect ascent. These words, even when descriptive of the
heavens, are always words of praise because they echo the praise constantly heard in heaven, as for example, "From Aravoth they praise and
from the firmament they bless." Because the text provides Ishmael with
instructions about ascent, it offers a rare opportunity to the scholar of
ritual texts to investigate how ascent is effected and how the recitation of
prayers and hymns contribute to the rite.

The complete text, as it now stands, seems to fall roughly into two
parts, one of which more or less surrounds the other. One part, a detailed
dialogue between Akiba and Ishmael, begins and ends *Maaseh Merkabah*.
Here, in essence, Ishmael asks Akiba about the means of attaining heavenly visions – "How is it possible to catch sight of" – and Akiba replies
with reports of what he has seen in previous ascents and of the formulas
he spoke during these trips. In the lengthier and more complex sections
that interrupt the Akiba-Ishmael dialogues, Nehunya teaches Ishmael the
language of the heavenly realm – prayer, names and letters – telling his
student to recite what the heavenly creatures recite: "When you pray,
recite the three names that the angels of glory recite." In the course of
this complicated central dialogue, Nehunya also teaches Ishmael to sum-
mon an angel while other angels discuss the "mysteries" with Ishmael.

The text consists entirely of reported speech: speech of individual rabbis, angels, and heavenly choruses. The cast of characters talks. Not only is the entire text "talk," but the subject of their dialogue is modes of speech. They outline and discuss what is heard in heaven, for these words are the proper ways of speaking – to be successful in ascent. The text is brimming with examples of the indigenous ideology of language use. In outlining the ascent process, the text reports not deeds but various verbal actions: "Akiba said: he prays a prayer," or "He [Nehunya] said to me: When you pray, recite the three names . . ." The understanding of ascent in *Maaseh Merkabah* is based on special modes of language use, a use that implies ritual efficacy.

Speech reported in *Maaseh Merkabah* always is attributed to a specific character. Sometimes it moves through several layers of attribution (Ishmael said . . . I asked Akiba . . . he said . . . Purity is in his heart and he prays); sometimes it is more simple (Akiba said). But often the message or final goal of the reported speech is a hymn. Such hymns can be easily distinguished from the dialogic frames in which they are embedded; all are highly parallelistic, highly repetitive formulaic recitations of praise. Sometimes they are familiar from the rabbinic liturgy, as for example "holy, holy, holy is Adonai of hosts, he fills the whole earth with his glory" (Isaiah 6:3). At other times, they consist of dense praise phrases, repeated and slightly altered.

> Blessed in heaven and on earth
> Glorified in heaven and on earth
> Compassionate in heaven and on earth
> Holy in heaven and on earth

Some other sections combine the word "name" with nonsense words:

> Blessed is your name alone
> LBDW Z<WM WDSWM . . .

Each of these levels of speech within speech, of rabbis quoting rabbis who recite hymns that in turn quote the divine chorus, reports an instance of language actually being spoken and all are associated with ascent. In sum, in the process of ascending, each individual talks about ascent. The text thus constantly reflects back on itself, explicitly talking about the very process toward which it is directed.

What have scholars made of this cryptic and often startling text? The scholarly debate about this text in large part has been set by the agenda of Gershom Scholem, who edited the Hebrew text and included it in his corpus of Hekhalot (palace) or Merkabah (chariot) texts.[5] Scholem's critical agenda highlighted two issues, both of which remain controversial: the date of the texts and their "normative," experiential nature. He consistently argued for a Late Antique (first-fourth century) date for these texts, even though the manuscripts date from the medieval period.[6] He argued that religious speculation of the first centuries A.D. provides the best context for understanding the texts and their worldviews. He amassed a multitude of parallels that help to illuminate the texts and also hunted out references to esoteric speculation in both Greek and Christian literature datable to the first centuries.[7]

Scholem did not try to date specific texts. He tried to compile enough Late Antique parallels to the texts to shift the burden of argumentation to those who supported medieval dates. Scholem clearly showed that many of the themes from the Hekhalot texts were evident in the early centuries A.D., including a heavenly chorus, restricted esoteric investigations, and ideas of ascent. However, he failed to convince scholars that any of the specific texts he edited already were known in that period in the forms in which we now have them.

Dating these texts is complicated by several factors. The texts are known principally from later medieval manuscripts and, therefore, cannot be dated on paleographic grounds. As a group, they contain few historical references; the very nature of the texts makes them difficult to date; they portray timeless lessons. All the texts are composites, showing signs of editing and redaction. Each is a version containing expanded sections, intrusions and duplications. Rarely are we dealing with an "original."[8]

Morton Smith (1963) correlated references to events in the apocalyptic sections of *Hekhalot Rabbati* with the rabbinic system of dating and concluded that these sections of the text were from the mid-fourth century. The hymnic sections of the text, however, remain undated. More recently Alexander has settled for the vague statement that "All things considered, then, though 3 Enoch contains some very old traditions and stand in direct line with developments which had already begun in the Maccabean era, a date for its final redaction in the fifth or sixth century A.D. cannot be far from the truth" (1983, 229).

While no one currently accepts Scholem's pre-Christian dating, none of the rest of rabbinic literature is pre-Christian either. Refinements in the dating process may result from analysis, rather than being a prior necessity for analysis.[9]

In addition to dating, Scholem compared the texts with other ascent texts raising the second problem. What kind of texts are these? He saw the texts as evidence of an early experiential ascent practice, which only later degenerated into an exegetical procedure. The ascent practitioners were indigenous to Judaism. Indeed, they were the same rabbis known from other rabbinic texts and not a fringe of heretics or madmen. To highlight the experiential nature of the texts, he compared them to ritual texts including "theurgic" and "magic" rituals. For example, he compared elements of the Lesser Hekhalot to the Greek magical papyri in terms of the similar "theurgical descriptions and prescriptions and the accompanying ever increasing number of magical names and Ephesia grammata" (1965a, 75).

At the same time, in his quest to place these strange texts at the heart of Judaism, he balanced his magical characterization with an emphasis on the normative (i.e., talmudic) character of the texts. Scholem cited talmudic passages concerned with hymnology, highlighting the normative character of the texts by their similarities with "normative" hymns.[10] Subsequent development of these conceptions in the early Medieval period then would be seen as a natural outgrowth of native Jewish concepts and not the result of borrowings. If the Jews shared theurgic practices with other religions, at least the Jews had them first.

In the end, for Scholem, the ill-defined notions of magic, normative religion, and gnosticism all collapsed.

> Indeed, the speculative, religious elements in these remains of the Hebrew and Aramaic Hekhalot books is so closely interwoven with the magical ones, that I feel the distinction drawn by many scholars today between Gnostic literature proper and that of the magical papyri is somewhat overstated (1965a, 75)

Scholem's heirs are still struggling with this problem, rejecting Scholem's characterization of Merkabah mysticism yet failing to supply an alternate model.[11] The only consensus to emerge in recent scholarship is that textual editions should not mask over the multiple textual problems and variants.[12]

Ascent as a Ritual Practice

Taking into consideration all of Schaefer's warnings about the textual evidence, one is still left with the problem of how to proceed. Once the synoptic versions are presented, how can one begin to construct arguments about the goals of the texts, the modes of composition and arrangement, and how can one bring greater precision to Scholem's attempts at comparison?

Scholem's multiple parallels do not begin to solve the problem of the form and functions of the hymns; the variety of comparative material is simply too broad. He describes the treatment of hymns in the text as "unusual" because "the very same hymns are characterized by the text as representing two different types of songs" (1965a, 20): the first type recited by the heavenly creatures, and the second by the individual who ascends. This is "unusual" seemingly because the same hymns operate as divine praise (religion) and as ascent liturgy (magic).[13]

The function of the Hekhalot hymns shifted depending on the particular parallel he was drawing. When Scholem stressed the magical parallels, the hymns worked by magic; when he stressed the talmudic parallels, they were liturgical and functioned "liturgically." Scholem bequeathed this problem to subsequent scholars. Gruenwald argues that the hymns can be divided into two kinds: ecstatic (containing nonsense) and nonecstatic (standard liturgy). The presence of standard liturgy such as the Alenu[14] in a mystical text raises questions, as Gruenwald implies, about the connection between the content and compositions of hymns and their possible functions (1980, 182).

The second kind of hymn is distinguished from the standard prayers in that it includes "magical and theurgical voices:"

> In this respect they resemble the magical prayers, the ἐπαοιγαι, of the magical papyri. In tone and structure these "prayers" also resemble the hymns of the Hekhalot Rabbati, the only difference being that the latter do not contain the lists of magical names. It may thus be argued that the "prayers" of Maaseh Merkabah are the only ones of their kind that so clearly expose their theurgical function.[15] (1980, 182).

His discussion is very preliminary, but raises the problem, for example, of whether a standard prayer becomes a means of theurgy simply by its placement in a Hekhalot text. In order to advance this discussion, it is necessary to introduce greater precision about the function of verbal formulas. Is the "function" of a prayer located in its internal structure and tone or simply in its placement within a larger text? Also, is it possible to distinguish among theurgic hymns, prayers, and magical incantations based on the structure and the tone? What, specifically, is the connection between the forms of these compositions and their functions within the rites?

Morton Smith, comparing the technique of ascent portrayed in *Hekhalot Rabbati* and that of the "Mithras Liturgy," labels the hymnic materials *spells*, stating that they are "songs, of course, like the Latin Carmina and the Greek epodai" (1963, 124). Yet, his only comparison with the Greek Mithras Liturgy is purely thematic. The reason for his comparison of the hymns to Carmina is not explained. As to the role of these compositions, he states that they "enable their possessor to not only ascend to the highest heaven and see the Throne, but also to know the future and the secrets of men's mind and enemies will be blasted" (1963, 142). He does not articulate why they function thus, except to state that "their virtues are all we should expect" (1963, 142).

We can turn in two directions here, toward theories of liturgical prayers or toward theories of magical language. Liturgical language has been the focus of limited study, with the important exception of Larry Hoffman's article "Censoring in and Censoring out: A Function of Liturgical Language." Hoffman attempts to refine theories of liturgy by introducing a more detailed linguistic analysis. According to Hoffman, the study of liturgy too often is concerned only with the censoring aspects of liturgical formulas. The addition or deletion of certain phrases in liturgy is related to polemical aims of the group, the aim of establishing clear group boundaries by the willingness or unwillingness of individuals to assent to these creeds. Although Hoffman believes that prayer can and does function in this manner, he challenges "the general notion that liturgical decisions are akin to catechetical statements, and that liturgical recitation is equivalent to theological polemic" (1981, 22). Too much attention is given to the creedal aspects of prayer and the extent to which liturgy is shaped in opposition to outsiders. "Liturgical language is thus conceived (according to this scholarly paradigm) as serving primarily to convey a factual, even polemical message to the worshipper, generally about some political or theological principle that we hold but they do not" (1981, 21).

Hoffman is correct that this understanding of prayer will never explain the role of liturgy, which presumably has dimensions distinct from theological speculation. Instead, Hoffman argues that in rabbinic prayer, the "rhythmic word flow" is more important than the semantic meaning of the words (1981, 25). Analysis of these compositions begins not with the meaning of the words and phrases, but with the repetitive structures of their composition. For example, he observes that several different kinds of phrases serve as substitutes for each other, occuring in similar places within the larger structure. These include (1) announcements of praise (Blessed are you); (2) object of praise (creator of the world); and (3) a temporal clause (forever and ever) (1981, 27). From this, he concludes that they are structurally equivalent and that many phrases are viewed as equivalent because their meanings are secondary. Instead of having meaning, the words "all point to the same master image, they may be used interchangeably and even strung together rhythmically to function like a mantra in suspending ordinary consciousness" (1981, 30).

Hoffman's contribution is in reopening the question of the function of language by pointing out that words do not always operate in the same manner. He thus has altered the dimensions of investigation, striving to refine the debate about the role of these hymns by introducing technical terms from linguistics, such as *semantic*. His careful review of the limitations of semantic analysis, based on the complex structures of hymns, illustrates the necessity of an expanded linguistic analysis of the text. What functions can words fill other than the commonly used semantic ones? In particular, he posits a trance-inducing function, predicated upon the notion that repetition of structural equivalents leads beyond semantic values by suspending consciousness.

Hoffman's analysis, however, cannot account for the particular literary patterns that he mentions. If the text is used simply to induce a trance, why are the structures so complex; why is the same word not simply repeated over and over? The limitations of his analysis are caused by one of Hoffman's basic assumptions. He equates structural equivalence with semantic meaninglessness. For example, if several phrases occur in similar places within the larger text, this "structural equivalence" deprives them of semantic value. However, the fact that there are several ways of saying the same thing, or that several different phrases replace each other in the same position in the text, does not mean that they are all meaningless. Consider, for example, a dictionary, which lists possible replacements or equivalent substitutions for a word. Here it is understood that structural equivalence leads to heightened or more precise semantic meaning and not to the opposite, semantic meaninglessness.

Hoffman is correct in his critique of the limitations of previous scholarship. The study of liturgy has often been based on a narrowly-defined theory of the function of words, as evidenced by the lack of studies that deal explicitly with this subject. However, there has been extensive debate about the role of words in anthropological and linguistic circles.[16] Some of these studies, along with insights from literary analysis of hymnic texts, may provide us with alternatives to Hoffman's equation of structural equivalence and semantic meaninglessness. In particular, the search for meaning should neither be confined to nor completely abandon semantic meaning, narrowly conceived, in favor of a broader analysis of the functions of language. Hoffman began his study because he felt that present studies of word functions in liturgy were conceived too narrowly. We, in turn, hope to find a theory of language functions that, unlike Hoffman's, does not begin with the semantic-meaninglessness of ritual language.

Analyzing Nonsense: A Functional Approach to Language

The other possible direction, as noted earlier, is toward studies of magical language. Magical language until recently has been understood as working literally by magic; that is, as performing its function in some turbid, impenetrable ether apart from everything normal – and allowing no further study. However, anthropologists have greatly expanded their notions of how words can be used and have developed more precise means for describing the social functions of language. In the case of *Maaseh Merkabah*, the selection of a functional approach is motivated by several of the most striking characteristics of the text. First, the speakers align the recitation of verbal formulas with articulated results. In the process of introducing the hymns, the speakers imply that the uttering of these words is connected with an anticipated outcome. The very first speaker, Rabbi Ishmael, chooses as the topic of his question the role of verbal formulas and, thereby, begins the investigation into the functions of language. Akiba states that, when he spoke, he had a vision of the heavenly world, and elsewhere instructs Ishmael that when he prayed a prayer, he was delivered. Thus, native to the text are notions that language has a transforming capacity and that words can be spoken in order to bring about, or effect, certain processes.

Second, as layers of reported speech, the conversations serve to introduce or "frame" the hymns. Because we see the hymns "in action," being uttered by the speakers, these frames serve not only to introduce the topic of the hymns but also to establish the contexts of use for those hymns. That is, by presenting the hymns in use, the frames of these hymns

proved explicit examples of context, which only a functional approach
can examine and perhaps explain. This mode of organizing the text reinforces the first characteristic discussed: not only does the verbal sequencing (I said → I saw) imply language as goal-directed, but also the forms
(reported speech) found in the text contribute examples of such language
uses. For example, Akiba presents the first formula with the instruction,
"purity is in his heart and he prays a prayer" indicating that in order for
the words to operate correctly, in addition to knowing the words, the
speaker must also have a pure heart. The use of reported speech shifts the
text from a discussion about the perceived efficacy of language to examples of such efficacy. Thus, methods selected must be appropriate to a
text that is not merely discussion about ritual speech but that consists of
examples of ritual speech.

Third, by exhibiting intricate arrangements of sound, words, and
phrases, the formulas are examples of poetry. This poetic structure warrants consideration of the poetic function of language. A suitable method
must describe, for example, the role of parallelism. When Akiba describes
the heavens, he lists them one by one from the lowest to the highest,
enumerating the number of chariots in each heaven. He uses the exact
same phrase to describe each layer, simply increasing the number of chariots in each layer. His words create, as it were, a picture or image of the
heavens, as he piles up phrases in the same manner in which the heavens
are piled up. Therefore, we need a means of locating and explaining these
images and other arrangements found throughout the text. Indeed, sections of the text include nonsense words that have no semantic value and
whose presence and purpose in *Maaseh Merkabah* therefore cannot be
explained by semantic investigation. Motivations for these clusters may
be found by consideration of the poetic functions of language.

The theory of poetic text pragmatics developed by Silverstein (1981;
1984) supplies methods appropriate to *Maaseh Merkabah*, for his theory
introduces greater precision into the discussion of language functions by
differentiating between two general types of function. The first function
includes those linguistic usages recognized by the speakers as purposive
uses.[17] Examples include questioning, declaring, and naming. As noted,
Maaseh Merkabah is replete with verbal activities; the speakers enact these
activities in connection with the successful completion of the ascent ritual. For this reason, the study in part focuses on ideas and notions about
the functions of language that are native to the text; that is, the ideology
of language use exhibited and discussed by the speakers.

The second type of functionality is that based on the relationship between language forms and their contexts of use. This includes the way in which language forms are dependent on their contexts, as well as the way in which forms entail or create their contexts.[18] In other words, native ideologies of language use do not fully account for the complexity of language function (1978). There are dimensions to the relation of forms to their contexts and to the transformational power of language, of which the users may be less aware. Thus, an exhaustive analysis will include, but not be limited to, indigenous notions of language use. For example, transformational dimensions of ritual language implicated by the poetic function of language may operate distinct from native ideology.

Silverstein's study of poetic structure is influenced by the work of Roman Jakobson on parallelism. According to Jakobson, parallelism is not connected only with couplets, it is the basic artifice of verse. He begins his famous article on parallelism: "We must consistently draw all inferences from the obvious fact that on every level of language, the essence of poetic artifice consists in recurrent returns" (1966, 399).

As such an omnipresent device, parallelism extends to all linguistic levels and forms. Recurrent returns include all repetitive patterning from phonetics to grammar.

"Pervasive parallelism, inevitably activates all the levels of language, the distinctive features, inherent and prosodic, the morphological and syntactical categories and forms, the lexical units and their semantic classes in both their convergencies and divergencies acquire an autonomous poetic value" (1966, 423).

The basic unit of analysis is the entire composition, for the pattern extends throughout the text. Parallelism is not merely a device for altering or extending the meaning of one line in the text nor a means of highlighting delimited rhetorical effects of paired lines.

This focusing upon phonological, grammatical, and semantic structures in their uniform interplay does not remain confined to the limits of parallel lines but expands throughout their distribution within the entire context. The significance of such distribution lies in Jakobson's definition of the poetic function, according to which "equivalence is promoted to the constitutive device of the sequence" (1960, 358). In other words, patterning of linguistic units results in multiple comparisons that are an intrinsic part of the message. The repetition of words and other linguistic units creates comparisons and contrasts, which are the creative aspects of poetry. Words and other units that occur in the same relative place in several layers of the parallel structure are, to that extent, literally, juxtaposed one with another.

"Phonetic features and sequences, both morphological and lexical, syntactical and phraseological units, when occurring in metrically or strophically corresponding positions, are necessarily subject to the conscious or subconscious questions whether, how far, and in what respect the positionally corresponding entities are mutually similar" (1966, 399).

Thus, for example, the juxtaposing of words creates glossing or defining relations between the words, which contributes to the meaning of words in the context of the composition.[19] According to this mode of analysis, structural equivalence (similar relative placement), contra Hoffman, contributes to meaning, including semantic meaning, and does not negate it. For example, in the line "Blow, bugle, blow, echo, dying, dying, dying," the repetition of the word *dying* does not make the word meaningless. Instead, the arrangement of the words provides an image (a diagrammatic icon) of the dying echo of the bugle. This repetition supplements the semantic value of the word and introduces another, nonsemantic, type of meaning.

Silverstein has taken Jakobson's insights and incorporated them into his theory of poetic text pragmatics. The meaning of a ritual composition is located in part in the internal structural relations of the composition, because the arrangement of words and other units is motivated by the goals of the ritual (1981).

Silverstein focuses in particular on the structural layers extracted from the text in much the same way as Jakobson would analyze and highlight the interconnecting patterning of any poem.[20] According to Silverstein, these patterns are important in as much as they are guides to the manipulations of the ritual. These structures provide diagrammatic icons (images) of the context of the rite. When, for example, Akiba enumerates the number of fiery chariots in each of the heavens, the context for the ritual of ascent is evoked and established.[21] The process is similar to the creation of the image of the dying echo mentioned earlier but, in this case, the image is related in its particulars to the ritual. The diagrams that underlie ritual texts, because they are about the situations of use, serve in part to create and manipulate the ritual context. In other words, utterances, just like clothing, locations, etc., can serve to establish the proper context for a ritual.

The transformational power of ritual language is effected through the transformation of these diagrammatic icons. The diagrams are manipulated by the literary devices, such as parallelism, that appear sequentially in the text, demonstrating transformation by the very flow of discourse. Or, to put it another way, the ritual text taken as a whole is transformative in that the accomplishment of the rite establishes a context that presupposes the effected rite. The text creates a situation in which the rite has already been completed.[22]

The language of a ritual text fills a double role. On the one hand, it indicates (indexes) that a specific transformation is occurring, for it presupposes and entails the transformation. At the same time, the composition of the text, the arrangement of patterns of words and other units, provides explicit information about the transformation occurring. It creates an image of that transformation. When, for example, Akiba states, "When I ascended to the first palace I was pure; when I ascended to the second palace, I was holy," etc., the piling up of heavens is a diagrammatic icon of the heavens themselves and juxtaposing the ethical values marks out the inner changes. Each of these changes has occurred when the individual moved to a higher level.

We can now more carefully define why *Maaseh Merkabah* is indeed a ritual text. What qualities of the texts was Gruenwald trying to capture when he used the term *manuals*, and why have these texts elicited debate about their exegetical versus experiential nature? Clearly, the ritual dimension stems in part from the fact that these texts include commands, which indicate practice. *Maaseh Merkabah*, however, unlike the magical papyri, does not outline step-by-step "recipes" for effecting desired ends. If, for example, we only counted imperative forms, much of the text would fall outside the purview of the investigation. Instead, in this text, ritual formulas are presented by means of models. Rabbi Akiba instructs his student and the reader by demonstrating the use of the formulas. The forms of the text (intricate patterns, dense phrases) can only be understood in terms of their contribution to the ritual goals. On the one hand, usages of language in the text imply that language is effective, that the words of the hymns are "performative" (Austin 1962; compare Silverstein 1978). Just as the verb *promise* means that an act of promising is taking place, so, too, the performative words of this text tell us that an ascent is taking place; to say X is to ascend. At the same time that the words are words about the ritual transformation, they also are models or diagrammatic icons of that transformation. This means we learn not only that a transformation is occurring, but also exactly what that transformation is. As Akiba lists the heavens, changes that transpire as he travels through them are examples of that transformation. This understanding of ritual language explains not only the semantic content of the ritual language but it also addresses, as already noted, the problem of the nature of ritual language. Words are arranged in intricate ways because the "message" of these patterns informs us about the goal of the text. The uses of language in the text are understandable. Words will not be viewed as semantically meaningless only if the text is viewed as an example of the indexicality and diagrammatic iconicity of ritual language. That is, the text presents effective words and also provides a model of the exact effect sought and achieved.

This study, then, will first review the ideologies of language presented in the text in an attempt to locate what might be called a native pragmatic ideology. How do the speakers think words function? To anticipate some of the findings, the rabbis believe that the deity's name has a special power. In addition, when the deity speaks, his words have a special power as well, as they learn from the creation story in Genesis. In fact, retelling or interpreting the creation story appeared to be a widespread means of presenting theories of how language operated. The story is replete with possibilities, and the rabbis were not alone in seeing the story as a basic source for information about the power of language. If God created the world through speech, what lessons do exegetes draw from the story about the creative potential of language? Any theory of language, of powerful language, must also include notions about the relation between words and object and how it is that words have meanings. We therefore also will survey notions about the sources of meaning and general ideologies of language, again to highlight the particular configuration of *Maaseh Merkabah*. In the final chapters, the rabbinic ideology will be compared with linguistic forms found in the text. For example, we will be looking for connections between ideas about language and the use of reported speech, and even nonsense words. Simultaneously, we also will investigate the creativity of linguistic forms, operating as devices for achieving transformational goals of the text. It may also be possible at that point to make some general observations about ritual language and use our findings to critique current scholarly theories of how ritual language works.

The goals of this analysis are clearly delimited. It is an attempt to see if there is order and purpose to the seemingly random organization of this complex text. If it is possible to enumerate the linguistic poetic manipulations, and then to describe their employment, the underlying structure of the compositions will become clearer. Many forms found in *Maaseh Merkabah*, such as reported speech and parallisms, are found throughout rabbinic literature. Very little work, however, has gone into understanding their functions in the texts. If it is possible to connect their roles with the goals of the ritual, to show why certain forms are placed within the text, the organization and composition of the text will be seen as purposeful. Establishing a connection between linguistic patterns and pragmatic goals illuminates the appropriateness of the text. Following the lead of Hoffman, we are trying to find the motivation for text composition, employing our expanded notion of meaning, which includes pragmatic as well as semantic meaning.

Two possible challenges to the applicability of a pragmatic approach relate to the text's status as (1) a contextless text that cannot easily be located in a specific historical community and (2) a composite text edited from more than one source. As to the first objection, as already noted, the immediate contexts of use for the formulas are described by the frames that introduce them. That is, the text does not simply present the formulas with no indication of the correct manner in which to employ them. Instead, the frames give examples of the proper setting; indeed, they make the formula into an exact instance of its use. It is as if the formulas carried their context with them, when Akiba states "as soon as I prayed this prayer I saw 64,000 myriads of angels of glory. . . . It is upon me to praise." However, there also is the issue of the context more widely conceived; that is, the historical setting in which the text operated. It could be argued that because pragmatic analysis imports notions of socially understood language functions, it is necessary to have evidence external to the text to support any interpretation. Such evidence would help to articulate the socially understood beliefs, and thereby lend validity to the interpretation of a particular text. In this regard, the work of Silverstein on Chinookan tales (1984) becomes especially important, for there he investigates just such "contextless" texts. The import of his article is to show that the manner in which verbal patterns of interaction are exemplified in a text reflects socially understood patterns of interaction. It is possible to use the texts as evidence of the socially shared conceptions because the constructions encode the cultural conceptions. The text in and of itself is evidence that can be decoded because language in part creates its own context of use, whether it is spoken or reported speech.

In the case of *Maaseh Merkabah*, the text is not primarily narrative, composed as it is of speech and speaking constructions, and thus even more obviously is context creating. The native ideology of the text, however, is quite distinct and influences the particular conceptualization and employment of verbal strategies in the text. To anticipate a point, the native ideology presumes that the name of the deity has a special power, a theory that will have far-reaching effects on the form and content of the text. Here, it is indeed useful to have external evidence that such a theory is found in other rabbinic texts, and a brief survey of such evidence will be conducted.

As to the second objection, the composite nature of the text theoretically could disqualify it. That is to say, an analysis of some composite texts might fail to progress, if the literary forms and their arrangements in the text had been disturbed or incompletely preserved. The justification of the use of these procedures must then be demonstrated by the outcome. At this point, the claim can only be made that the composite nature of the text does not preclude analysis. Instead, many paragraphs that have been combined in the text reflect different tactics but similar general strategies. We have sufficient examples within the text to discover the forms. Even if we are dealing with a composite text, we can view it as an example, or perhaps a composite of examples, of the portrayal of ascent and the appropriate language.

As an example of this much broader circle of texts, *Maaseh Merkabah* seems particularly suited for a functional investigation for some of the reasons already mentioned. While other Hekhalot texts would reveal other examples of ritual language and the use of literary devices, *Maaseh Merkabah* has several advantages. The text contains no major interruptions such as the extensive apocalyptic sections in *Hekhalot Rabbati*, which would necessitate raising another set of interpretive issues. In addition, because the text is cast as reported speech, the formulas that it presents are explained in part. The formulas presented are the object of discussion for the speakers who report them. These speakers provide introductions to the formulas that articulate the uses and situations of use. Thus, the text creates its own commentary, which cannot help but supply us with guidelines for our investigation of the functions of the formulas. We can study the issue of the native use of language because, in part, it is so directly commented on and outlined in the text.

CHAPTER TWO

Introduction to the Text

The Text's Coherence, Date, and Place of Origin

No narrative or story line ties the text together.[1] In *Maaseh Merkabah*, the "plot" is generated by the questions Ishmael asks and the shifting topics of discussion. In the beginning and ending sections of the text, Rabbi Akiba[2] teaches Rabbi Ishmael[3] ascent hymns and describes his own experience of heavenly visions (sections 1-6, 8-10, and 32-33). When Akiba depicts ascent in response to Ishmael's inquiries, he recites hymns of praise and sketches out the heavenly realm, incorporating enumerations of the heavens cast as a series of repeated phrases.

The intervening sections present more than one procedure: Rabbi Nehunya[4] teaches Ishmael the procedure for summoning the Prince of the Torah and Ishmael attempts it (11-15), Ishmael learns to recite lists of angel names (21-23/26), and finally Ishmael employs ascent hymns "arranged" for him by Nehunya (26C-31).[5]

Angelic characters are introduced with no explanation of their roles, which presumably the reader already knew. These include the Prince of the Countenance,[6] the angel of the Countenance, the Prince of the Torah, and the Prince of Gehenom (see Table 1). Angelic discussion introduces secondary themes of ascent. For example, they discuss who is privileged to make use of the "secret," unlike the more single-minded discussion of ascent between Akiba and Ishmael.

One factor, though perhaps a weak one, that lends coherence to the text is the appearance of Ishmael in twenty-four of the sections.[7] Ishmael's

Table 1. Characters, Actions and Divine Names in Maaseh Merkabah

Section	Characters	Action	Heavenly Characters
1	Ishmael Akiba	questions Akiba gives prayer	RWZYH Adonai, God of Israel
2	Akiba	describes ascent vision	
3	Ishmael He (Akiba)	questions (Akiba) describes ascent visions	TRQYLYY Adonai, God of Israel YH WṢ YH Adonai, God of Israel
4	He (?) Ishmael (or he) Akiba me (Ishmael?)	questions Akiba gives prayer summarizes instructions gives prayer	RWZNYM Adonai, God of Israel ZRYZ Adonai, God of Israel RZYY Adonai, God of Israel RWZYY Adonai, God of Israel
5	Akiba	gives prayer	GRWYY Adonai, God of Israel
6	Akiba	describes ascent vision gives prayer	GHWZYY Adonai, God of Israel
7	Ishmael Nehunya	describes ascent vision	
8	Akiba	describes ascent vision	BRWKYY Adonai, God of Israel Ṭ<NṬRGB Adonai, God of Israel

9	Ishmael Akiba	questions Akiba describes ascent vision gives prayer	
10	Ishmael Akiba	questions Akiba describes ascent vision	>NPQ> Adonai, God of Israel
11	Ishmael Nehunya	reports dialogue gives instructions for summoning angel	SWRY Prince of the Countenance YWPY>L Prince of the Torah SQDH NBY>Y angel of the Countenance SQDHWZYHW your servant
12	Ishmael	reports dialogue	>RPRS angel of the Countenance gives names
13	Ishmael Nehunya	questions Nehunya gives names and letters	prince of wisdom B>RKM Adonai, God of Israel
14	Ishmael	uses names	PYWYQRT angel of the Countenance PRQRM angel of the Countenance PRZM angel of the Countenance
	Ishmael PNQRS Adonai, God of Israel	reports dialogue	PNQRS Adonai, God of Israel
		warns Ishmael	PWQRS Adonai, God of Israel

Section	Characters	Action	Heavenly Characters
15	Ishmael	seals self with names	PDQRS Adonai, God of Israel
16	Ishmael Nehunya	reports dialogue gives mystery, names, prayer	MQLS >SGDṬṢṢ (names of beasts?)
17	Ishmael Nehunya	questions Nehunya instructs to pray	
21	Ishmael Nehunya	reports dialogue describes ascent vision	
22	Ishmael	report of dialogue (Nehunya mentioned)	princes of wisdom
23	Ishmael	gives names	SWWRY>L Prince of the Countenance ZHRY>L Adonai, God of Israel ZRZRY>L angel of the Countenance SNDLPWN (Sandelphon)
24A	Ishmael ZBWZY>L angel of the Countenance	reports dialogue (mentions Akiba) questions Ishmael	ZBWZY>L angel of the Countenance
24B	Ishmael ŠQDHWYD angel of the Countenance	reports dialogue chides Ishmael	ŠQDHWYD angel of the Countenance

25	Ishmael	gives formula, mentions ŠQDHWYH angel of the Countenance	
26A	Ishmael Nehunya	reports dialogue questions Ishmael	
26B	Ishmael Nehunya	reports dialogue gives mystery	
26C	Ishmael (emended) Nehunya	reports dialogue	
27			Z<WPY>L Prince of Gehenom Adonai, God of Israel (variants: YHDYY Adonai, God of Israel)
31B	Ishmael Nehunya	reports dialogue explains role of prayer	
32	Ishmael Akiba (emended)	reports dialogue gives formula	
33	Ishmael Akiba	questions Akiba gives prayer	RWZYY Adonai, God of Israel RWZYY Adonai, God of Israel

first question – what prayer a man says ascending to the chariot – broadly conceived is the theme of the entire text. In addition, the text is linked together as a whole by the similarity of sections 1 and 33. In the last section (33), Ishmael asks to see over the head of the seraphim who stand over the head of RWZYY, Adonai, God of Israel. In effect, he is asking to see above the seventh heaven, repeating but altering the question from section 1 and using the same divine name. Presumably the verbal composition given in section 1 permitted viewing the "top." Therefore, compliance with the new request in section 33 establishes a new hierarchy that subordinates all prior sections. By offering the corresponding prayer, Akiba extends the ascent to yet another level and thus completes the whole text as well.

The independence of the sections is by no means unique to this text. In fact, the opposite seems to be true: one of the characteristics of these texts is juxtaposing of many discrete units that carry on general themes but display potential variation in arrangement and sequencing. For example, Alexander writes about *III Enoch*,

> It is evident, however, on closer investigation, that III Enoch has arisen through the combination of many separate traditions: it tends to break down into smaller "self-contained" units which probably existed prior to their incorporation into the present work. In the process of being brought together these preexisting units of tradition were accommodated to each other only minimally, and so the work contains not a few cases of overlapping, inconsistency, and even contradiction. (1983, 223).

The coherence of the text is in large part due to the coherence of these individual units. In the case of *Maaseh Merkabah*, the smaller "self-contained" units are themselves constructed from several types of material. The formulas are built with bits of praise and descriptions of the heavenly world and, in particular, of the chorus. The other major type of building block is the reported speech frames, which ground the formulas by presenting their purposes and functions. The sections are combinations of these smaller parts, and the sections themselves are arranged, loosely connected by theme or procedure. Because it is possible for the reader to understand each section – this is praise; this is a description of heaven – the text is readable and usable, if not seamless. The composite nature of the text stems from the nature of the Hekhalot texts, which share, reedit, and adapt sections from disparate sources. The introductory frames provide a very important "glue." Rewriting the frame may be sufficient to integrate a unit with the material around it, making it a part of the same dialogue, or monologue, as the preceding or subsequent sections.[8]

The text is written in Hebrew, similar to the other Hekhalot texts.[9] A few Aramaic phrases in the angel-summoning procedures are woven into the very fabric of the formulas although they appear to be instructions as to how the recitation should be carried out.[10]

As to the date of the text, a few comments should be added to the previous discussion.[11] When Odeberg tried to posit an early date for *III Enoch*, stating that it pre-dated the talmudic parallels,[12] Scholem countered by stating that this text in fact was one of the later ones.[13] He outlined his own progression of Hekhalot texts, with the Lesser Hekhalot placed at the beginning as one of the oldest examples. He supported this contention by pointing out that "the Aramaic of the text is old and genuine, the dialect Babylonian" (1941, 45). He also mentions that Akiba instead of Ishmael is the central character, as if that also supports an early dating (1941, 45).

Unfortunately, he supplies no evidence for these arguments, and it is by no means proven that either the appearance of references to Akiba or the Aramaic language are evidence of the date. Similarly, Scholem traces a development from the use of the term *employment of the glory*, which, around the beginning of the sixth century changed to *descent to the chariot* (1941, 46-47). This argument in particular might be of some help in dating *Maaseh Merkabah*, where this term appears, but again Scholem has failed to supply evidence for his contention.

Alexander's attempt to date *III Enoch* includes a careful review of several previous arguments and, in the process, surveys the range of ways prior scholars had tried to fix a more definite date for these elusive texts.[14] He examines each of Odeberg's points and concludes that two of them are especially central: (1) that *III Enoch* cannot be later than the material in b. Hagigah 11b-16a; and (2) that *III Enoch* is earlier than the other Hekhalot texts. Although he accepts these two points, he turns them around completely and argues that both are evidence of a late instead of an early date. He then settles on the conclusion that the text can be dated from the fifth to the eleventh century. Alexander has made two important contributions in this discussion: he has shown the extent to which such arguments are circular; and he also has demonstrated that we may have to settle for dates that span centuries. To complicate matters even further,

Alexander believes that the final form of the text reflects the work of a school and not a single author, though he does not discuss this issue in any detail (1983, 228).

In the process of criticizing prior attempts to date *III Enoch*, Alexander disqualifies all arguments that simplistically connect a theme with a historical event. In the end, he opts for dependence, either the dependence of other texts on *III Enoch* or vice versa. We cannot easily develop better criteria for dating *Maaseh Merkabah* and, since we have no evidence of dependence, we must settle for a very unsatisfying conclusion. The next step would seem to be a more careful study of all the Hekhalot texts, so that if no absolute dating can be developed, it might at least be possible to create a relative dating schema, showing which Hekhalot texts are likely to be dependent on other Hekhalot texts. Dating may best be split into two distinct aspects. *Maaseh Merkabah* contains material that is as old as *III Enoch* and other Hekhalot texts,[15] although the redaction process may not have been finally completed until centuries later.

Although the manuscripts stem from European circles,[16] the Hekhalot texts are presumed to have come originally from Palestine and Babylonia.[17] In some texts, the presence of Babylonian or Palestinian Aramaic may indicate origin, though Scholem notes that Medieval copyists tended to substitute the more familiar Babylonian forms for the Palestinian (1965a, 76). As with the dating problem, the few remarks Scholem makes about the specific origins of texts are not as well developed as we would wish. For example, he remarks that the presence of Greek elements, as in the magical words, points to a Palestinian origin (1965a, 31). Greek elements, however, also could be found in Babylonia.

Maaseh Merkabah contains no hints of "local color" or references to places in Palestine. In terms of vocabulary, at this point in the investigation of the Hekhalot texts, no standards have been developed for judging origin by means of word choice.[18] The story of Ishmael's fast and subsequent lesson from Nehunya is set in the temple in *Merkabah Rabbah*, but in an unspecified location in *Maaseh Merkabah*. If the purpose of the text is to teach the rite to any "man," the phrasing of the text may be as "locationless" as possible and any items that might seem to limit the text to specified places, including both Palestine and Babylonia, have been excluded. A Babylonian origin seems more likely, in part because of the greater development of Hekhalot themes in the Babylonian Talmud.[19] This by no means implies that the final redaction and compilation took place in Babylonia.

The Ideology of the Divine Name

"You spoke and the world existed/ By the breath of your lips you established the firmament" (lines 850-851)

"Creator of his world by his one Name/Fashioner of all by one word" (lines 1095-96)

The incorporation of creation summaries, as witnessed in these two citations, signals the ideology of language of *Maaseh Merkabah*; God's "breath," his Name, functions in special ways. This is not a surprise, for Hebrew exegetical literature abounds in statements about the power of the divine Name.[20] Especially prominent are prohibitions against uttering the divine Name and the names of other gods, as well as anecdotes about the power of the Name and its use by the deity in creation.[21]

These ideas are not attested in the Hebrew Scriptures. While there are injunctions against the improper use of God's name, Hebrew Scriptures contain no prohibition against merely stating it.[22] Similarly, while the creativity of God's word is found in a few scriptural references, nowhere does it explicitly state that the deity created the world by speaking his Name.[23]

The source of these ideas is not immediately clear. Egyptian "name-magic" is sometimes cited as the source of the creative use of the divine Name, following the lead of the Talmud itself.[24] The Name as an instrument of creation seems to be first connected with an oath containing the divine Name that was used to seal creation. According to Fossum (1985, 245-253), the sealing by means of the name was a reinterpretation of an earlier cosmogonic myth. Scriptural references to the deity's word, as in Psalms 104:7, where the deity does combat by means of his "rebuke," are reinterpreted to be by means of his name. For example, Enoch asks to learn the hidden name from the oath by which "The heaven was suspended before the creation of the world" (Enoch 69:14-25).[25] In the *Book of Jubilees* 36:7, Isaac exhorts his son to "swear a great oath, for there is no oath which is greater than it by the name glorious and honored and great and splendid and wonderful and mighty, which created the heaven and the earth and all things together."[26] Similarly the Prayer of Manesseh states, "He who bound the sea established it by the command of his word, he who closed the bottomless pit and sealed it by his powerful and glorious Name."[27] None of these citations contain anything close to the elaborate divine Name ideology which will develop, though they are the clearest precursors.[28]

These themes about the prohibitions and power of the divine Name are developed in a series of anecdotes found in widely disparate Jewish texts.[29] No single rabbinic text includes all of the anecdotes we will survey about the divine Name; subplots include its restriction, its use in creating the world, and its use and abuse by Israelites, biblical figures, and individual rabbis.[31] The particular articulation of the theme depends on the other points the story is trying to make.

The strongest possible punishment is meted out for its use, loss of a portion of the world to come.[32] In other cases, stories are told that the Name can only be transmitted to certain people (sages) under certain restrictions. According to b. Kiddushin 71a, the Name was taught only by sages to their students, and even sages were restricted from uttering it.[33] B. Avodah Zara 17b recounts the punishment of Hananiah ben Teradion, who taught his disciples the divine Name.

The only other uses of language that elicit similar injunctions are the uttering of the names of other gods, of blessings, and of curses.[34] Already in the Hebrew Scriptures, blessings and curses are automatic and irrevocable, much as the use of the Name will later become.[35] Invoking the deity to bless or curse someone is the closest parallel between human speech and the powerful speech of the deity and may have been a partial model for the developing name-ideology. As we will see, however, it is the divine Name that becomes the focus of the most intense interest and the greatest creative power.[36]

The sealing of the abyss of creation by the Name as mentioned above, is found in *Hekhalot Rabbati* 23 and in Makkot b. 11a, where a shard with the Name written on it is thrown into the abyss to hold back the waters that threaten the entire world.[37] Sometimes, creation is caused by one or two letters of the Name.[38] B. Berachot 55a attributes to Rav the idea that Bezalel knew how to combine the letters by which heaven and earth were created.[39] Genesis 2:4 and Isaiah 26:4 are interpreted as proof that one letter of the divine Name was used to create this world and another was used to create the world to come (*Pesikta Rabbati* 21).

Exegetes composed an entire "history," or rather a series of sometimes contradictory histories, describing the role and function of the divine Name in human events.[40] The distant past and the future were both portrayed as times when many people knew (or would know) how to use the Name.[41] The history of the Name became a metaphor for the presence of the deity on earth and the interaction of the deity with his people. For example, one story tells that the Name was once entrusted to the entire nation, given to them during their journey through the desert. It was taken away, however, due to their worship of the golden calf.[42] Numerous stories recount how usage was restricted to holy places (the Temple) and holy people (priests).[43] Perhaps the most famous or widely cited "history" recounts that, at one time, knowledge of the Name was widespread but, due to the growing corruption of human society, usage was continually restricted culminating in almost complete restriction after the death of Simon the Righteous (b. Yoma 39b; cf. j. Yoma 40d, iii, 7). The Name itself was diminished; after the destruction of the Temple it consisted of two letters (b. Er. 18b). The "present" state of the world is such that prayers are not heard because they do not include the Name (*Midrash Psalms* 91.8).[44]

A particularly rich anecdote that reveals linguistic ideology states that the divine Name is not to be uttered in court by a witness. Even in a situation where an individual is not himself intending to speak the Name, but is merely reporting someone else's use of it, the witness is still perceived to be using the Name.[45] This ideology is explored further by examining whether any word used to refer to the deity is, in fact, a Name and thus prohibited. The extension of punishment for blasphemy, even to those who substitute divine attributes for the Name, implicitly argues that even these Name substitutes still refer to the deity and therefore qualify as Names.[46]

The power of the divine Name is illustrated by stories of its use by biblical figures, demonstrating that its power was not confined to the single act of creation. The Name was used for protection and even offence by these heroes. Solomon used a ring with a divine Name on it to subdue Ashmodei (b. Git. 68b).[47] Moses used it to kill an Egyptian (Exodus Rabbah on 2:14). Pesikta deRav Kahana 19 answers the question what did the sea behold? by stating that "It beheld the divine name graven on Aaron's staff and fled."[48]

The divine Name also is used in several stories to animate lifeless images, a variation on the creation theme. Abraham created "living souls" by this means.[49] Jeroboam's golden calf was animated by the Name, which was placed in its mouth (b. Sota 47a). Nebuchadnezzar made an image live either by placing the priest's breastplate with the Name on it into the mouth of the image or by writing the Name on its forehead. Daniel removed the Name and the image became lifeless again.[50]

If the Name was generally "lost," a few stories describe its use by individual rabbis. The most detailed story in the Talmud is the creation

of a calf by two rabbis using the divine Name. The story is told twice
(b. Sanh. 65b/67b) and was subject to extensive subsequent elaboration.[51]
Finally, the Name used to create the world also received a Name, the
Shem Ha-Meforash (the explicated/detailed Name).[52] After reading the
translation, we will examine the particular ideology of the divine Name
in *Maaseh Merkabah*.

CHAPTER THREE

Translation and Notes

The text used as the basis for translation is New York 8128 as edited by Schaefer. Variant readings from the other four manuscripts are included in the notes.[1] There are two sets of notes: (1) numerical citations in brackets are used for the textual variants found at the end of the translation and (2) numerical citations without brackets are used for additional comments at the bottom of the page. Annotations include

( )   possible derivations for the letter manipulations and extra English words needed for clarity of translation

< >   superfluous letters, such as when the copyist began a word twice and a few corrupt additions that disrupt syntax

/ /   Emendations, made only where (1) New York was untranslatable or apparently incomplete and therefore deemed corrupt and (2) the other manuscripts offer a better reading that is closely related to the New York reading

Three additional notations have been taken directly from Schaefer, and appear in the translation exactly where they appear in the text.

**   crossed-out letters and words

[ ]   textual additions from above the line glosses that appear in the margins

The numerical notations signifying variants are placed exactly where the variants appear if possible. Otherwise the prior or subsequent word and/ or phrase is mentioned. The inclusion of variants is not meant to be a first step to a critical edition, though some of the variants do stand out as better readings. Instead, it is meant at this stage to highlight the types and breadth of variation, for it supplies a rough notion of the kinds of differences displayed in the manuscripts and their distribution.

Possible explanations for the variations differ depending on the type of divergence. Some of them may be due to scribal error. In the case of the angel names, letter manipulations, and letters signifying numerical values, there is wide variation due in part to the difficulties of transcribing the material. These elements are easy to confuse and precision in copying is not to be expected, particularly in the case of "nonsense" words. Additionally, the repeated use of the same words and the piling up of similar phrases may also lead to errors caused by skipping from word to word or phrase to phrase.

Second, where all manuscripts vary, it may reflect a general obscurity in the text. Where, for example, three of the four manuscripts exhibit different readings, it is as if each copyist had opted for a different way of construing an unclear passage. Each of the speaking frames is internally consistent in the main, but the particular speaking situation varies among the manuscripts (to him/to me). The levels of embedding (X said . . . Y said) can be easily confused, due to the complexity of the discussions, so that copyists may have developed differing interpretations of the exact dialogue.

Third, some of the variants are created by the individual "style" of the copyist. For example, M 22 tends to expand the formulas, adding "he fills the whole earth with his glory," where the other manuscripts include only the first half of the sanctification formula. N 8128 peculiarities include the construing of parts of the divine names as words (lines 302, 884) and the development of a more standardized introduction for the prayer sequence (27-31) by the addition of the word "five" to line 836 and the subsequent labelling of each prayer ("The first, etc. prayer").

In several instances, I have decided that N 8128 is corrupt and that it is worthwhile to emend the translation based on the other versions. From the hundreds of variants, only a small number fit the criteria to warrant emendation. N 8128 has to present a problem such as an untranslatable word in the midst of an otherwise clear phrase or the incomplete presentation of a repeated or stereotypic phrase. In addition, all the other manuscripts had to contain the same alternate reading, which was either clearer or more complete.[2] Usually, the N 8128 version is easily recognizable as a minor variant of the other versions. In each case, where N 8128 is emended, the emended words are bracketed // so that it is immediately apparent that the words are not from N 8128. In addition, the N 8128 reading is included in the notes.

0001   *Section 1 [Scholem] (Paragraph 544 [Schaefer])*

0002

0003 R. Ishmael said:

0004

0005   I asked of R. Akiba a prayer that a man does when ascending

0006 to the Chariot[1] and requested from him praise[1] of RWZYH

0007 Adonai, God of Israel, who knows who he is, and he

0008 said to me:

0009   Purity and holiness are in his heart and he prays a

0010 prayer:

0011 Let you be blessed[2] forever on the throne of glory.[2]

0012 You dwell in the chambers of the heights and in the place of sublimity.

0013 Because you revealed the mysteries/and the mysteries of mysteries[3]

0014 and the secrets and the secrets of secrets

0015 to Moses and Moses taught them[4] to Israel

0016 so that they would be by means of them doers of Torah,

0017 and would make great by means of them learning (literally, Talmud).[3]

0018

0019   *Section 2 (Paragraph 545)*

0020

0021 R. Akiba said:

0022   When I ascended and caught sight[4] of the Mighty One I

0023 observed all the creatures which are in all[1] the pathways of

0024 heaven, and their upward length and their downward

---

1. Compare the opening of *Hekhalot Rabbati*: Rabbi Ishmael said, "What are the songs someone says who wishes to view a glimpse of the chariot? (Schaefer, p. 40, paragraph 81).

2. The hitpael form used here (TTBRK) functions as an imperative. This form and the third person (YTBRK, may he be blessed), are found throughout rabbinic liturgy and may reflect a specific ideology of blessing. The reflexive aspect, for example, may stem from the notion that all blessing ultimately comes from the deity. In the context of this study, however, a complete investigation is not possible.

3. Cf. *Merkabah Rabbah*, paragraph 675-76 (Schaefer).

4. The verb *catch sight* (ṢPT) frequently refers to a vision of the heavenly realm. It also appears in sections 4, 6, 8, 17, 21, 31, and 33, though not in section 9 as recorded by Alexander (1983, 255). Cf. *Hekhaloth Rabbati*, paragraphs 81, 83 (Schaefer).

0025   width and their upward width and their downward
              length.[2]/5
0026
0027   *Section 3 (Paragraph 546)*
0028
0029   R. Ishmael said:
0030   How do the angels of service stand upon them?[6]
0031   He said to me:
0032   Like this[1] bridge that rests over a river. And the whole
0033   world passes over it. Thus rests the bridge from the
0034   start until the end of the passage, and angels of
0035   service circle on it and sing a song before
0036   ṬRQYLYY Adonai, God of Israel, and
0037   zealous ones of awe, captains of fear stand before[2] (him),
0038   thousands of thousands of thousands and
0039   myriads of myriads of myriads[7] and give praise and
0040   extoll before the /throne/[3] of YḤWṢYH Adonai, God
              of Israel
0041
0042   How many bridges (are there)? How many rivers of fire?
0043   How many rivers of hail? How many storehouses of snow?
0044   How many wheels of fire? How many angels of service?[4]
0045   (There are) twelve thousand myriads of bridges,
0046   six above and six below;
0047   Twelve thousand /myriads of/[5] rivers of fire,
0048   six above and six below.
0049   Twelve thousand myriads of rivers of hail,
0050   six above and six below.
0051   Twelve thousand myriads of storehouses of snow,
0052   six above and six below.
0053   Twenty-four myriads of wheels of fire,
0054   Twelve above and twelve below.
0055   And they encircle the bridges, the rivers of fire,

5. The size of the creatures is discussed in greater detail in section 10. These sections are reminiscent of Shi'ur Komah (measurement of the divine body) texts. For an introduction to this material, see "Shi'ur Komah," *Encyclopedia Judaica*, 14: 1417-19. See also Alexander 1983, 241, n. 60.

6. Cf. *III Enoch* 22b-c and the haggadic fragment included by A. Jellinek 1937, vol. 6, 153-54.

7. Cf. lines 124-27.

0056   the rivers of hail, the storehouses of snow,

0057   the angels of service.

0058

0059   How many angels of service are in every passage?[8]/[6]

0060   And every creature, they stand in its midst

0061   opposite all the pathways of heaven.

0062

0063   *Section 4 (Paragraphs 547-549)*

0064   /And what does RWZYY Adonai God of Israel (do)?/

0065   He said to R. Ishmael[1]

0066   How is it possible to catch sight of them and see what

0067   RWZNYM Adonai God of Israel does?[9]

0068   R. Akiba said to me:[1]

0069   I prayed a prayer of mercy

0070   and by this means I was delivered,

0071   God ZRYZ (zealous) Adonai God of Israel.

0072   Blessed are you, God great, mighty in might.

0073   <And what *I did* does> and I was able to catch sight of them

0074   and to see what the RWZYY Adonai God of Israel does.

0075   And therefore listen to what R. Akiba said to me[1] and

0076   revealed [to me] in order that every person who has in

0077   his heart the praise of RZYY Adonai God of

0078   Israel, this great /mystery/[2] is being revealed to me.

0079   He will complete it every day at sunrise and will wash

0080   himself from sin and from wrong[3] and from every evil[10] and

0081   RWZYY Adonai God of Israel deals with him

0082   righteously every day in this world and stands on

0083   his behalf for his glory and secures for him that he

---

8. Alexander (1983, 305), who notes that as it stands the text is unclear, translates the (W) *and* instead as the notation for the number *six*, and reconstructs the version of this sentence in *III Enoch* as follows: How many ministering angels are at each entrance? Six for every single human being, and they stand in the midst of the entrances, facing the paths of heaven.

9. See *III Enoch* 22B and the haggadic fragment included in Jellinek, 1937, vol. 6, 153-54.

10. This is a rare occurrence of a command that is not limited to verbal actions, and is one of the few instances in the Akiban sections where an individual is told to perform a ritual action other than the recitation of a formula. Even in this case no specifics about washing are given, and the washing from sin may be an inner purification. That is, the instructions fail to include specifics – where to wash, how often – found in instances of such instructions in other texts.

0084	is a son of the world to come.[11]
0085	And this is the prayer:
0086	/God/ RWZYY Adonai God of Israel
0087	Blessed are you Adonai God great in might.
0088	Who is like you in heaven and on earth?
0089	/Holy in heaven[4] and holy on earth./
0090	He is a holy king, he is a blessed king.
0091	He is a king distinguished over the entire chariot.
0092	You stretched out the heavens, you established your throne.
0093	And the great name is adorned on the throne of your glory.
0094	You laid out the earth,
0095	You established in it a throne as a footstool for your feet.
0096	Your glory fills the world.[5]
0097	Your name is great and mighty in all might.
0098	And there is no limit to your understanding.
0099	You know the mysteries of the world.
0100	And investigate wisdom and hidden paths.
0101	Who is similar to you, probing hearts
0102	and investigating inner thoughts and understanding thoughts?
0103	Nothing is concealed from you.
0104	And nothing is hidden from your eyes.[6]
0105	All life and death, blessings and curses,
0106	Good and evil are placed in your hands.
0107	And your name is distinguished in heaven and on earth.
0108	The greatness of your power is in heaven and on earth.
0109	Blessed in heaven and on earth.
0110	Glorified in heaven and on earth.
0111	Compassionate in heaven and on earth.[7]
0112	Holy in heaven and on earth.
0113	Zealous is the remembrance of your name
0114	forever and forever and forever
0115	until the end of all generations.
0116	This is your name forever
0117	And this is your remembrance for generation and generation.
0118	Merciful and compassionate[8] is your name.
0119	Your compassion is mighty for the ones above and ones below

---

11. The phrase *son of the world to come* seems to be a technical term for an individual who has successfully ascended. As such, it may provide some hints as to the goal of ascent.

0120   Good are your words for the lovers of your Torah.

0121   Pure are your utterances for those who sanctify your name.

0122   Your ways[9] and your paths on water[10] you established.

0123   Your throne is in power and might, song and chant.

0124   Clouds of fire, zealous ones of awe, captains of fear,

0125   thousands of thousands of thousands

0126   and myriads of myriads of myriads[12]

0127   give praise and extollation

0128   to your name, great, mighty and awesome.

0129   Before you stand all the mighty ones.

0130   For they declare distinguished in praise and in chant.

0131   In the chambers /of Torah/, in the storehouses of blessing.

0132   From Aravoth[13] they praise and from the firmament they bless.[11]

0133   From here blessing and from there /praise/.

0134   Who is a God like you,

0135   pardoning sin and forgiving transgression.

0136   Who is there in heaven who has strength to do your deeds and your mighty acts?

0137   Your mighty acts are fire, [your] chambers are fire.

0138   You are fire, consuming fire,[14]

0139   And your throne is fire, TNWTYK is fire and your servants are fire.

0140   /Your name/ is hewn in flaming fire.[12]

0141   ḤY YH YHW holy and awesome.

0142   Blessed are you, Adonai distinguished

0143   <blessed, distinguished> in the chambers of song.[13]

0144

0145   *Section 5 (Paragraphs 550-51)*

0146

0147   R. Akiba said:

0148   As soon as I prayed this prayer I saw 640 thousand

0149   myriads of angels <of service> of glory who stand opposite[1] the

---

12. Cf. lines 37-39.

13. *Aravoth* appears in other texts as the name of the seventh heaven (b. Ḥag. 12b), though that does not seem to be its function here. In this case the term is a general way of refering to the upper realm.

14. God is called a consuming fire in Deut. 4:24. In this case, however, an additional (H) has been added to the end of *consuming* (>KL), the purpose of which is unclear. Cf. *III Enoch* 42:4 where "consuming fire" is clearly identified as a name of the deity.

0150   throne of glory and I saw the knot of the tefillin[15] of
0151   GRWYY Adonai God of Israel and I gave praise in
0152   all my limbs.[6]
0153   It is upon me to praise the Lord of all.
0154   To proclaim the greatness of the creator of the beginning.
0155   Who has not made us as the nations of the earth.
0156   And has not placed us as the clans of the ground.
0157   Who has not placed my share among theirs and my lot as the multitudes.
0158   For they bow down before vanity and emptiness.
0159   And pray to a god who does not save.
0160   And I pray to the king of kings of kings, the Holy one, Blessed is He.
0161   Who stretched out the heavens, and founded the earth.
0162   And the presence of his strength is in the high places of the heights.
0163   He is our God and there is no other one.
0164   Truth is our king and there is none like you.[2]
0165   Adonai he is God, Adonai <God> he is God, Adonai he is God.
0166   He is one and his name is one.
0167   Adonai is our God, Adonai is one.
0168   Adonai, Adonai, God of mercy and compassion,
0169   slow to anger and great in loving kindness and truth.
0170   For this reason we trust in you, Adonai our God,
0171   That we will soon see the royal tribute of your strength,
0172   so as to wipe out idols from the earth
0173   and the false gods will be cut down
0174   so as to repair the world in the kingdom of Shaddai
0175   And all people who will call on your name
0176   To turn toward you all the wicked of the earth.
0177   They will recognize and will know, all who dwell on earth,
0178   that to you every knee will bend and every tongue will swear.

---

15. For the deity taking off his tefillin, see *Merkabah Rabah* 655 (Shaefer).
16. The "Alenu" became the standard closing prayer in rabbinic liturgy. This prayer, which is built from images from Jer. 10:6–16, Is. 30:7, 35:23, 51:13 and Deut. 4:39, is ascribed to the third century authority Rab (R. H. 1:3. 57a, A. Z. 1:2, 39c). The standard form has never been dated. The prayer was clearly aded to the text, as the changes from the plural to the singular demonstrate (*It is upon us* to *It is upon me*). Cf. Scholem 1965a, 105.

0179 And every person standing before you, Adonai our God, will bow and fall down,

0180 to the glory of your name they will give dignity.

0181 And all of them will accept the yoke of your kingdom.

0182 And you will become king of them soon, forever and ever.

0183 because it is your kingdom

0184 And you will be king forever in glory[3]

0185 and I will sanctify your name

0186 great, and mighty and awesome,

0187 Holy, holy, holy Adonai of hosts, the God great, mighty and awesome,

0188 majestic, distinguished, wonderful and glorified.

0189 HDYRYRWN,[17] true, great, pure, detailed[18] is your name,

0190 hewn in flaming fire which lives

0191 HY YH YHW YHW holy and awesome.

0192 Blessed are you Adonai, distinguished in the chambers of song.[4]

0193

0194

0195   *Section 6 (Paragraphs 554–55)*

0196

0197

0198 R. Akiba[1] said:

0199 Who is able to meditate on the seven palaces

0200 /and to catch sight[2]/ of the heaven of heavens and to see the

0201 chambers of the chambers and to say I saw the chambers of

0202 YW?

0203

0204   In the first palace stand four thousand myriad[s][3] of

0205 chariots of fire and two thousand myriads of flames

0206 are interspersed between them.

0207

---

17. This word may be a confused form of *distinguished* (>DYR) combined with *lofty* (RM).

18. The root (PRŠ) *detail* occur in one of the most famous "names" for the name of the deity, the Shem Ha-Meforash, the explicated/detailed name. This term is found, for example, in San. 7:5, and contrasts with "nickname" (KYNWY). Cf. b. Sotah 38a; Can R. 1.4; PRE 37 end; Pesik R 14; and "Shem Ha-Meforash," *Jewish Encyclopedia* 11:262–264, Chapter 5, pp 164–66 and Janowitz 1989.

0208   In the second palace stand one hundred thousand
0209   /myriads/ of chariots of fire and four thousand
0210   myriads of flames are interspersed between them.
0211

0212   In the third palace stand two hundred thousand myriads
0213   chariots of fire and a hundred thousand myriads of
0214   flames are interspersed between them.
0215

0216   In the fourth palace stand a hundred and four thousand
0217   myriads of chariots of fire and four thousand
0218   myriads of flames are interspersed between them.
0219

0220   In the fifth palace stand four thousand thousand
0221   myriads of chariots of fire and four thousand
0222   myriads of flames are interspersed b[e]tween them.
0223

0224   In the sixth palace stand a thousand thousand thousand
0225   myriads of chariots of fire and two thousand thousand
0226   myriads of flames are interspersed between them.
0227

0228   In the seventh palace stand a hundred thousand
0229   thousand myriads of chariots of fire/and two thousands
0230   thousand myriads of flames are interspersed between them.[4]
0231

0232   In the first palace chariots of fire say:
0233   Holy, holy, holy is Adonai of hosts.
0234   He fills the whole earth with his glory.
0235   And their flames of fire scatter[5] and gather together
0236   toward the second palaces and say:
0237   Holy, holy, holy is Adonai of hosts,
0238   He fills the whole earth with his glory.
0239   In the second palace chariots of fire say:
0240   Blessed is the glory of Adonai from his place.
0241   And similarly their flames of fire scatter and gather together.
0242   toward the third palace and say:
0243   Blessed is the glory of Adonai from his place.
0244   In the third palace chariots of fire say:
0245   Blessed is the glorious name of his kingdom forever and ever
0246   from the dwelling place of his presence.

0247 And their flames of fire scatter and gather together
0248 toward the fourth palace and say:
0249   Blessed is the glorious name of his kingdom forever and ever
0250   from the dwelling place of his presence.
0251 In the fourth palace chariots of fire say:
0252   Blessed is Adonai, living and established forever and ever
and ever,
0253   distinguished above all the chariot.
0254 And their flames of fire scatter and gather together.
0255 toward the fifth palace and say:
0256   Blessed is Adonai, living and established forever and ever
and ever,
0257   distinguished above all the chariot.
0258 In the fifth palace chariots of fire say:
0259   Blessed is the holiness of his kingdom
0260   from the dwelling place of his presence.
0261 And their flames scatter and gather together
0262 toward the sixth palace and say:
0263   Blessed is the holiness of his kingdom
0264   from the dwelling place of his presence.[6]
0265 In the sixth palace chariots of fire say:
0266   Blessed is Adonai, lord of all might and
0267   Ruler over all the chariot.
0268 And their flames of fire scatter and gather together
0269 towards the seventh palace and say:
0270   Blessed is Adonai, lord of all might and
0271   Ruler over all the chariot.
0272 In the seventh palace chariots of fire say:
0273   Blessed is the king of kings,[7] Adonai, Lord of all might.
0274   Who is like the living and established God?
0275   His praise is in the heavens of heavens.
0276   The holiness of his kingdom is in the heavens of heavens.[8]
0277   His might is in the chambers of chambers.
0278   From here "Holy" and from there "Holy"
0279   and they bring song[9] continually
0280   and recite the name[10] of GHWZYY Adonai God of
Israel.
0281 And they say:

0282   Blessed is the glorious name of his kingdom forever and ever
0283   from the dwelling place of his presence.
0284
0285   *Section 7 (Paragraph 556)*
0286
0287   R. Ishmael said:
0288   When R. Nehunya ben Hakanah my teacher said to me[1]
            the mystery[2]
0289   of the chambers of the palace <and the palace> of the Chariot
            and also of the Torah.[3]
0290   I will not forget any chamber[4] of them – I saw the king of the
0291   world sitting on his high and exalted throne and all
0292   the ranks[5] of the sanctification of his name[6] and of his might
0293   sanctifying his name in his praise[7] as it is written.
0294   And this one called to that one and said:
0295   Holy, holy, holy is Adonai of hosts.
0296   He fills the whole earth with his glory.
0297
0298   *Section 8 (Paragraph 557)*
0299
0300   R. Akiba said:
0301   Happy is the man[1] who stands in all
0302   his power and bring[2] song before the cherubim[3] of
0303   Adonai God of Israel and who catches sight of the chariot and
            sees
0304   all things that they do before the throne of glory,
0305   on top of which sits BRWKYY (blessed) Adonai god of Israel
0306   and sees comandement and might and laws and good
0307   enactments that cancelled[4] harsh enactments from the
0308   world[19] and he will not/excommunicate/[20] his companion
0309   in the name[6] of Ṭ<N ṬRGB Adonai God of Israel because
0310   his name is like his might and his might is like his name
0311   he is his power and his power is him
0312   and his name is like his name.
0313   >ŠBWGG LMRŠ > BGD ŠSYGG GRW HG GDD HWZ
            NWR> (awesome)

---

19. On cancelling harsh enactments, see *Merkabah Rabba* 655 (Schaefer).
20. The import of this word is obscure, nor it is clear who *he* is, though presumably it is the deity.

0314 R<D HW> (he) SRBH Adonai <ḤD (one) >H HH YHW is
his name.[21]

0314

0316 *Section 9 (Paragraph 558)*

0317

0318 R. Ishmael said:

0319 I asked R. Akiba how many <how many> measures are thus[1]
between the bridges.[22]

0320 R. Akiba said to me:

0321 Were uprightness and righteousness in your heart

0322 then you would know how many measures are in heaven.

0323 He said to me:

0324 When I was in[2] the first palace I was righteous,

0325 in the second palace I was pure,

0326 in the third palace I was upright,

0327 in the fourth palace I was perfect,

0328 in the fifth palace I arrived holy[3]

0329 before the king of king of kings, blessed is his name.

0330 In the sixth palace I said the sanctification

0331 before the one who spoke and created and commanded[4] all
living beings.

0332 so that the angel[5] would not slaughter me.

0333 In the seventh palace I stood in all my power.

0334 I trembled[6] in every limb and I said:

0335 You[7] are the living and established God

0336 You created heaven and earth.

0337 Apart from you there is no rock.

0338 For eternity your remembrance will be praised by companies/
of above[8]

0339 The work of your hands is in the inhabited part of your earth.

0340 (The) great God, creator of everything.

0341 Lord[9] in greatness, loved in might.

0342 They confess before you the mighty ones of power

0343 Who stand[10] before you in truth, in justice.

0344 Justice you will manifest in your world.

0345 In the justice of your name you will save me.

---

21. This is the only occurrence of letter manipulations in the Akiban sections.
22. Cf. *III Enoch* 22C and the haggadic fragment in Jellinek, 1937, vol. 6, 153-154.

0346   And the blessing of your glory I will magnify for eternity.

0347   Blessed are you, distinguished in the chambers of greatness.

0348

0349   *Section 10 (Paragraph 559)*

0350   R. Ishmael said:

0351   I asked R. Akiba[1] how many measures are between the
        bridges?[23]

0352   He said to me:

0353   Between the bridges are twelve myriads of parasangs,

0354   in its ascent are twelve myriads of parasangs

0355   and in its descent are twelve myriads of parasangs.

0356   Between the rivers of awe and the rivers of fear[24]

0357   are twenty two myriads of parasangs.

0358   Between the rivers of hail and the rivers of darkness

0359   are thirty six myriads of parasangs.

0360   Between the chambers of lightning and the consoling clouds

0361   are forty two myriads of parasangs.

0362   Between the conclosing clouds and the chariot[25]

0363   are eighty four myriads of parasangs.

0364   Between the chariot and the cherubim

0365   are one hundred sixty eight myriads of parasangs.

0366   Between the cherubim and the ophanim

0367   are twenty four myriads of parasangs.

0368   Between the ophanim and the chambers of the chambers

0369   /are twenty four myriads of parasangs.

0370   Between the chambers of chambers and/[2] the holy beasts

0371   are forty thousand myriads of parasangs.

0372   Between the wings are twelve myriads of parasangs.

0373   And their width is similar.

0374   From the holy camps[3] to the throne of glory

0375   is thirty myriads of parasangs.

0376   And from the /foot/[4] of the throne of glory

0377   to the place on which sits the holy /king

0378   high/[5] and exalted, >NPQ> Adonai God of Israel,

---

23. Cf. *III Enoch* 22C and the haggadic fragment in Jellinek, 1937, vol. 6, 153-154.

24. The specific elements differ from those listed in section 3, sharing only the rivers of fire (cf. Daniel 7:10). Parasang is a Persian measure which equals approximately 3.88 miles.

25. Note that in the section there is only one chariot, as compared to the multiple chariots of fire in section 6.

0379   is forty thousand myriads of parasangs.

0380   And his great name is declared holy there.

0381

0382   *Section 11 (Paragraphs 560-62)*

0383   R. Ishmael said:

0384   I was 13 years old[26] and my heart was moved

0385   every day I was worn down in a fast. As soon

0386   as R. Nehunya ben Hakana revealed the Prince of the Torah,

0387   SWRY> Prince of the Countenance[27] revealed (himself)[1],

0388   he said to me:

0389   Prince of the Torah YWPY>L is his name and everyone who
seeks is revealed to me[2]

0390   him will sit forty (days) in fast,[28] will eat his

0391   bread with salt and should not eat any kind of filth.

0392   And he will /immerse/[3] immersions and not look at any

0393   kind of colored garment. His eyes <and> will be downcast to
earth.

0394   And he will pray with all his

0395   power and his heart will be concentrated[4] in his prayer

0396   and he will seal himself[5] with his sealing[29] and he will

0397   recite twelve words.

0398

0399   (561)You are God, living in heaven,[6] HHQWQ DSSYM
ṬWM

0400   ṬWWM ṬWM <Q<PWM <GBY BG>WH W<PSP>
ḤWKMT PRWF SRS PRṬT>

---

26. On the age 13, see Avot 5:24.

27. Gruenwald (1980, 184) construes this to mean that after Nehunya teaches Ishmael about the Prince of the Torah, Suria then talks to Ishmael and teaches him more about the Prince of the Torah. He seems to use the parallel from *Merkabah Rabba*, for this frame is not clear in its wording. On the name Suria, see M. Schwab, "Vocabulaire de l'angelogie," *Memories divers savants Academie des Inscriptions*, Ser. 1,10[2], 1987, p. 308. On the term Prince of the Countenance, or of the Divine Presence, see the note by Alexander, 1983 242-243. He states that the term is derived from Isaiah 63:9, "In all their affliction he was afflicted and the angel of his presence saved him." The term "angel of the presence," however, is not exactly the same as "Prince of the presence."

28. On these injunctions Gruenwald mentions Meg. 4:8, which discusses the wearing of colored garments before the ark. He also notes that according to several other citations, colored garments on women tempt men (cf. ch. 2:2). For a brief discussion of these injunctions, see his comments 1980, 185, n. 12. These references do not seem to have solved the ritual injunctions found in this section.

29. For sealing as a protective action, see Alexander 1983, 233.

0401   <GNYTYNTWN HDRTWP W>H BW?W
0402
0403   (Aramaic) And these are the seventy laws[30]
0404   he will recite DYMSP> BYH B>WH BDYR> YTHTM
          SWT PNY (face) >WT
0405   (sign) PYW >ṬWN YZZ ṬBY HDDYH prince of wisdom.
          And the
0406   seventy angels will descend near me. and ŠQDH NBY>Y the
          angel
0407   of the Countenance is with them. And he will recite
0408   the letters so that he will not be damaged. ZYYP
0409   PḤP ZRS ŠMP TWRG KKB PYMP YH to guard.
0410
0411   (562) You are God living in the heavens, who gave
0412   permission to the companies of your glory who will
0413   attend to people in purity.
0414
0415   I recite your name, which is one over all the
0416   living beings.
0417
0418   SBR DD>Y >DYR (distinguished) DRYRWN ḤPS
          DRSYY
0419   ḤWTM (seal) QDYŠ (holy) RŠ *QSY* QDŠ YHW BDP
          BR>YYH (creature)
0420   BRWK (blessed) L<WLM (eternal) <P M<WPP> YHW
0421   Holy and blessed is his name, seal above his head.[7]
0422
0423   Secret YḤRZ over the /secrets/[8] HGNBWB YH YHW YT
0424   They will sink[9] damaging evil ones from distinguishedness,
0425   and loftiness will bring a seal on his limbs.[8]
0426
0427   The distinguished ones of wisdom you created so
0428   that they have authority that they may bring down the
0429   secrets of wisdom by the authority of your name

---

30. Perhaps the "70 laws" are 70 names, as for example the 112 names in section 30. On drawing a circle on the ground, Gruenwald notes that while this is found widely in "magical" practices, this is the only occurrence of this injunction in the Hekhalot texts (*Apocalyptic*, p. 185, n. 15).

0430   because you are king of the world.

0431

0432   Thus I recite before you the name of SQDHWZ>Y your servant.

0433   QWWS DDY ZZ> ŠBRṢ WḤBY>L SGRṢ BḤR GY>L >RṬWWS

0434   NYLW MYPṬWN >RWṢ TRWM NQBWM TDQRWN ZRZW>L ZBWZY>L HGBṢ

0435   >DRṢ NSGYW>L ZRYW>L YHWH (Adonai) GDYTY>L YHWH (Adonai)

0436

0437   >L (God) YHY >LHY (God of)

0438   RZYYL> ḤYL> YHWH (Adonai) whose name is over the name of his creator,

0439   the name of SWDHWZYHW your servant

0440   I recited that there will be for him miracles and mighty act[s],

0441   many marvels, signs and wonders, great and

0442   awesome in the chambers of wisdom, and in secret[10] understanding

0443   and I will sing before you understanding

0444   as it is written:

0445   Who is like you among the gods Adonai?

0446   And there is no work like yours.

0447   Blessed are you Adonai, Lord of [miracles] and mighty acts,

0448   hearing the sanctifiers of your name

0449   and delighting in those who know your name.

0450   And he will lift up his eyes to heaven <and earth>[11]

0451   so that he will not die and will stand and recite (the) name

0452   and will adorn so that wisdom will be hewn

0453   on all his limbs and investigation of understanding in my heart[12] and

0454   he will proceed and he will pray in my name[13] and he will make[14] a

0455   circle (on the earth) and he will stand on the earth[15] so that the

0456   damagers will not come and whisper to[16] like angels and kill him.

0457

0458   *Section 12 (Paragraph 563)*

0459   R. Ishmael said:

0460   >RPRS the angel[1] of the Countenance said to me:

0461   Every one who wishes <a word[2]> to make use of this great mystery should pray

0462   it with all his power that he not forget one (word?)[3] If he forgot,

0463   all his limbs are in destruction. And he will call out those three

0464   names and I will descend: SDYR TYKRY >M YBY> BYHW SWWṢ >P RWP WYḤM.[4]

0465

0466   *Section 13 (Paragraph 564)*

0467   R. Ishamel said:

0468   I asked R. Nehunya ben Hakana, /my teacher,/

0469   how is the wisdom of the Prince of the Torah?[31]

0470

0471   He said to me[1]

0472   When you pray, recite the three names that the angels of /glory/[2] recite:

0473   ZṢ ṬWṢ ZRZY>L TYT TWPYṬY RB TQY?> >RWRY ZY>< <YZWZ RGBW

0474

0475

0476   And when you pray at the end recite the three *names* letters which the beasts

0477   recite when they catch sight of and see B>RKM Adonai God of Israel:

0478   GLY >YY >DYR >DDR YHY>L ZYK BNYB>.[3]

0479

0480   And when you pray another prayer recite the same /three/[4] letters which the

0481   wheels of the chariot recite, which say song before the throne of

0482   glory:

0483   HN PZ YP> PP Y>W GHW> SKYB>.

0484

0485   This[32] is the acquisition /of wisdom/[5] for which every person who reci[tes]

0486   acquires wisdom forever[6] and therefore a person can depend

---

31. On the Prince of the Torah, see Alexander 1983, 243. This figure seems to help individuals remember the texts that they study, or perhaps, know them without studying.
32. These lines are a mixture of Hebrew and Aramaic.

0487 on it. These are the three letters which Moses wrote [33] for Joshua

0488 on a /cup/[7] and he drank.

0489

0490   And if you cannot depend

0491 engrave them in an engraving and do not turn sideways

0492 from the words of the mighty ones.

0493 ZPQ QNYDR HWW W> HB> ŠBN QN ṬBB Ṣ BW HṢ HR YṬ HDRW HDR HWWH ŠKWN.

0494 And do not forget: >W QMP >WM WPYPY YD ZR >WR NWR,

0495 Awesome father, for zeal of wisdom and for distinction of understanding.

0496

0497   *Section 14 (Paragraph 565)*

0498 R. Ishmael said:

0499   I[1] sat 12 days fasting when I saw that I could [2] not (?)

0500 I made use of the [name][3] of the 42 letters[34] and

0501 PYWYQRṬ <and> the angel of the Countenance came down in displeasure.[4]

0502

0503   He said to me:[5] Emptyhead!

0504 I will not give over until you will sit for forty days.

0505

0506   Immediately I was frightened and[6] I recited

0507 the three letters and he went up:

0508 YH B>R<> BYH GDWLT >TYT BYH[35]

0509 and I sat 40 days and prayed[7] three prayers *three* at dawn three/prayers/at noon

0510 and three prayers in the evening and I recited 12 words over each and

0511 everyone and on the last day I prayed three[8] and recited /twelve[9] words/ and

---

33. In connection with the rare occurrence of a reference to writing, see also the use of *engraving* in line 491. The point of this line, and of the entire procedure, is obscure.

34. The 42-letter name is another of the well-known names for the deity. According to the Talmud (b. Kid. 71a), this name was only taught to those of good character. See the article, "Names of God," *Jewish Encyclopedia* 9:163

35. It appears that "letters" means groups of letters.

0512   PRQRM[10] angel of the Countenance descended,

0513   and with him the angels of mercy,

0514   and they placed[11] wisdom in the heart of R. Ishmael.[36]

0515   Who can stand at his prayer, who can catch sight of

0516   PRZM[12] angel of the Countenance[15] when he establishes this mystery?

0517   R. Ishmael said to me:[14]

0518   PNQRS Adonai God of Israel said to me:[15] Descend[16] and see a person like you.

0519   If he did not descend with authority,

0520   PWQRS Adonai God of Israel destroys you[17]/[37]

0521

0522   *Section 15 (Paragraphs 566-68)*

0523   R. Ishmael said: (With) seven[38] seals I sealed myself when

0524   PDQRS angel of the Countenance descended.

0525   Blessed are you Adonai who created heaven and earth

0526   by your wisdom and your understanding.

0527   Your name lives forever

0528   >YP SYSYP >YLWSS KYSY TNYY.

0529   (The) name of your servant[1] >WRYM SSTYY is on my feet.

0530   >BG BGG is on my heart.

0531   />RYM TYP> is on my right arm./

0532   LYBYY >RWM TYP> is on my left arm.

0533   >BYT TLBG >RYYN DWY>L is on my neck.

0534   >P >K QYṬR ŠM >HD (one) YDYD (friend) YD YH

0535   to guard my soul.[2]

0536   RYR GWG GDWL (great) TP YP HP THWR (pure) HHWS

0537   HHY HH HH HZ KRWT (I recited?) <WLM (eternal)

0538   Let you be blessed, lord of wisdom

0539   because all the might is your, it is.

0540   Blessed are you Adonai, lord of might,

0541   high and exalted, great in rule.

---

36. Here we would expect *me*. The *Rabbi Ishmael* may have originally been part of the next phrase, *R. Ishmael said*, and then shifted to the end of the prior phrase, displacing *me*.

37. Scholem comments, in his composite version of the text, that PDQRS the angel and PNQRS YWY God of Israel seem to be identical (1965a, 109, n.19).

38. The reason for the specific number is not made explicit, but it may correspond to the number of heavens.

0542	(567) You are king of kings of kings, blessed is he
0543	Let you only be blessed because you are one.[3]
0544	LHWKYH is your name.
0545	>WZWZ> W> DHWW ZWHWW >H is your name.
0546	DŠBY D>ZW is your name.
0547	>BYṢ YHZ is your name.
0548	ZYH > Y> ṬWR>W is your name <is your name>.
0549	GHWP is your name.
0550	<WṬṬH>H is your name.
0551	ḤBB WYŠ> is your name.
0552	LHBṬ GBRT RM is your name.
0553	ZH ZH ZYW
0554	Lord of the entire chariot,
0555	forever holy king let you be declared holy.
0556	Your holiness is in heaven and on earth.
0557	Blessed are you Adonai the holy God.
0558	(568) You are the king of glory.
0559	Your path is glory and your word is holy.
0560	Your name is great glory and holy forever, eternal forevers.
0561	RM (exalted) YHWW <<Z ḤYY GBWR (mighty) DRKY >RṢ (earth) RYW>H LK BRW>H WHRY Y>H HW
0562	BYHW >L (God) PB DRYRWN YR>H ḤKB> HH WWY> HṢ TM YTT HP P>R YHW YHW
0563	Let you, king of the world, be extolled because you gave permission
0564	for the recitation (remembrance) of/your/name,
0565	standing and sitting and in the rest of the magnitude of wisdom.
0566	YP ŠTT >DYH SBY >YP >R>H >P HPWK YWP>R BYP> NKṬR ḤYH HY ḤY Z> RM >DY >D (forever and ever)
0567	Let the king of praise be praised.
0568	because your name is great in praise and
0569	your name[4] is high and exalted.
0570	Blessed are you Adonai, great, living in might.[5]
0571	
0572	And I recited the three names[6] ZYYP PSP >RS (earth) from his
0573	name so that he would not approach me in destruction
0574	and when he ascended I recited the three letters so

0575   that the angels and the damagers would not touch me.
0576   RDNW YH> SHRY YW>Y >RBNY >YṢ TBY NZY W>
        H> HBW>
0577   ŠBYRT HMZYQYM (the damagers) RGBT BYNYYN
        >RYS MDRS QDWMH >LP >YS
0578   YH> YZ> (YW?) YWH MBY> >WP HP YH YD YH
        HW YH HW seal great.
0579
0580   *Section 16 (Paragraph 569)*
0581   R. Ishmael said:
0582   R. Nehunya ben Hakana said to me:
0583   A person who wishes to make use of this great mystery,
0584   let him recite the angels who stand behind the holy
0585   beasts MQLS >SGD ṬSS and let him pray a prayer that
0586   they will not/destroy him/ because they are more
0587   wrathful than all the hosts of the heights.
0588   And this is the prayer:
0589   Blessed are you Adonai, my God and my creator, holy[1] and
        awesome.
0590   Eternal life, /distinguished/ over the chariot.
0591   Who is like you, distinguished in the heights?
0592   Make me succeed in every one of my limbs.
0593   And I will speak out in the gates of wisdom.[39]
0594   And I will examine in the paths of understanding.
0595   And I will catch sight of/in the chambers of/ Torah.
0596   And I will recount in the /treasure-buildings[2]/ <because> of
        blessing.
0597   And they will be stored up for me because wisdom is before you.
0598   And save me from all the wrathful ones who stand before
        you.[3]
0599   And let them be friends to me before you.
0600   /And I will know/ that your holiness is forever.
0601   And I will bless the holiness of your name forever.
0602   And I will declare holy your great name.[4]

---

39. This formula is distinct from all the others in its frequent use of the imperfect. Perhaps the purpose of the formula in part accounts for this choice. The formula seeks protection and the tense structure implies that praise will be given to the deity if the request for protection is successful.

0603   And there will be a great seal on all my limbs of my body.
0604   As it is written:
0605   And this one called to that one and said holy, holy, holy is
         Adonai of hosts,
0606   he fills the whole earth with his glory.
0607   Blessed are you Adonai, eternal life.
0608
0609   *Section 17 (Paragraph 570)*
0610   R. Ishmael said:
0611   I asked R. Nehunya ben Hakana my teacher:[1]
0612   When one recites the twelve words[40] how /can/[2] one catch
         sight of
0613   the splendor of the presence[41]
0614   He said to me: Pray a prayer with all your power[3]
0615   and the presence is friendly to him[4] and gives him
0616   permission to catch sight and he is not damaged.
0617

Sections 18-20 Lines 618-711 are not included in this analysis. See
Appendix One, p. 115.

0712   *Section 21 (Paragrapha 579)*
0713   R. Ishmael said:
0714   R. Nehunya ben Hakana, my teacher, son of the
0715   proud said:[1] When[2] I caught sight of the vision of the
0716   chariot I saw a proud majesty,[3] chambers of chambers,
0717   majesties[4] of awe, transparencies of fear, burning and
0718   flaming, their fires fire[5] and their shaking shakes.
0719
0720   *Section 22 (Paragraph 580)*
0721   R. Ishmael said:
0722   As soon as I heard from R. Nehunya ben Hakana my
         teacher

---

40. The phrase *twelve words* occurs in section 11. Gruenwald attempts to use this section to tie together more closely the ascent ritual and the summoning of the angels. He interprets the question to be How can the person who is summoning the angels with the twelve words also have a vision of the deity? This is a tempting reading, for it does serve as a clear transition to the topic of ascent.

41. Scholem states that this term only appears in the sixth century, though he does not supply evidence (1941, 46-47).

0723   this announcement (literally hearing) *I heard* I got up and
0724   asked him all the names of the princes of wisdom and
0725   from the question that I asked I saw a light in my
0726   heart like the days of heaven (or broad daylight).[46]
0727
0728   *Section 23 (Paragraphs 581-2)*
0729   R. Ishmael said:
0730   As soon as I stood up and saw my
0731   face shining from my wisdom <and> I began to detail off
        each
0732   and every angel in each and every palace:
0733   In the first palace stand: ZHWPY>L and <ZPY>L,
        GTWRY>L and RṢ WṢ Y>L and
0734   SPṬ>L, BZT>L, <WZPY>L and <WZBBY>L.
0735   At the gate of the second palace stand: GBRY>L, TṢ PY>L,
        RHBY>L,
0736   ŠBZRY>L, ŠTQY>L, YHRBW>LL, <WKMY>L,
        <RP>L.
0737   At the gate of the third palace stand: HDRY>L, ZBDY>L,
        ZRWDY>L,
0738   SRW>L, <MT>L, <MNW >L, and <MTLY>L,
        ṬRDY>L and RWDY>L.
0739   At the gate of the fourth palace stand: SGSG>L, >SR>L,
        HYLWPY, and
0740   HYLWPTY, >LMWN, GLMWN, QDYŠ, HQSGDR,
        >Ṣ >GD>,
0741   BSWM, >KBMWS, PSWY, MDWR, GDRY>L,
        Z<WM, Z<H, >WR<WZRZ<Y
0742   At the gate of the fifth palace stand: DHRHY>L,
        >YDZD>L, DDGYT>L,
0743   GHṢ YṢ >Y, YṢ WṢ Y>L, DPYWN, HGY, ZYWY,
        PḤ Q, BY>L, BYS>L DKRWDY>L,
0744   G>L, >PQY>L, YYGR, YYQR.
0745   At the gate of the sixth palace stand: >BG BG, >SHSH
        >SPSP, HDSRGDF,
0746   RZWZY>L, <ṬWPY>L, GDGYT, SBS>L,
        HDWRY>L, S<N, DYRY>L, >YZY<Y>L,

42. Gruenwald translates this phrase as "light . . . comparable to the light of the first days of the creation of the world," which seems to be an over-translation (1980, 187).

0747   Z<Z>L, ṢZW<N>L, KRYQR>L, and <D>L,
SHSY>L, SWD>L, PSPSY>L, GHW>L, BYPY>L.

0748   At the gate of the seventh palace stand: >SMRYH, QMGMN,
>MYLPTWN,

0749   ŠMYNY>L, LPṬWN, QRTYYN, >BRY>L,
GDWDY>L, SRPSYWN, MLKY>L,

0750   >WPPY, LHBY, Z<Z<, ŠLHBYTH, ŠBYBY>L,
RYSPSYSY>L,

0751   >SPSY>L, G<G<, NY<WR, YQRTH, HPLY>,
MWPLY>L,

0752   and SWWRY>L Prince[1] of the Countenance, who sees
the image of

0753   ZHRY>L Adonai God of Israel. (582) And above all sits
the king

0754   of the world[2] on his throne, high and exalted. And

0755   angels of glory rejoice in songery and shouters of

0756   shouts and narrators of his might[3] stand on his

0757   right and on his left.[4] And these are their names:

0758   <YGYWN, <DY>L, >S??Y>L, SBWSY>L, and
>YBWRY>L, >SKNYZB>L,

0759   GDWS QSP>L, PSBW>L, >GRGRDY>L, <ZRY>L,
<WZRYN, <S,

0760   and PPY, NGD, GHYDY>L, GHWDR, ZRZDY>L,
HDRWTY>L, and MQYP,

0761   >DR GHW, and D>W, YWPY, and PSYNGD,
GHWDY>L, GHDYY,

0762   ZRZRY>L angel of the Countenance and SNDLPWN
binds tefillin[52] on

---

43. According to *Hekhalot Rabbati* 14:4, to know the names of angels is to know how to invoke them. The names of angels in part derive their significance from the understanding that they include in them the name of the deity (cf. Exodus 23:20ff). For the name Suriel, see Schwab, "Vocabulaire," p. 308. In *Hekhaloth Rabbati*, Nehunya sends Ishmael to see Suriel when Rome begins a persecution against some of the elders (5:5).

44. This section appears to contain two "tops;" ZHRY>L Adonai God of Israel in line 753 and then the Eternal Rock Adonai God of Israel in line 763. Sandalfon is a famous angel, who appears widely in angelic texts. See Schwab, "Vocabulaire," p. 313 and the article "Sandalfon," *Jewish Encyclopedia* 11:39-40. The standard derivation for the name is from the Greek, meaning "brotherly." See also b. Hag. 13b and PesikR 20 (ed. Friedmann, p. 97A) where Sandalfon binds crowns of praise on the head of the deity. This is also the line cited by Eleazar of Worms from a text entitled *Maaseh Merkakbah*, which led Scholem to choose that title for his edition (Scholem, 1965a p. 112, n. 23).

0763   the head of the Eternal Rock Adonaia God of Israel, let his
0764   name be blessed. God, great, mighty and awesome,
0765   distinguished and eminent, strong, powerful. God
0766   proclaimed wonderous, exalted, who sits on the wide
0767   places of the heights[4] and does his will in the world
0768   and no one can alter it.
0769
0770   *Section 24 (Paragraphs 583-84)*
0771   And[1] R. Ishmael said:
0772   ZBWZY>L the angel of the Countenance said to me:
0773   Son of the proud, what[2] is
0774   the privilege of your father and mother that you
0775   obtain the privilege to stand on this mystery that all[3]
0776   the world is not privileged?
0777   And I and R. Akiba are privileged to make use of it
0778
0779   (584) R. Ishmael said:
0780   ŠQDHWYH the angel of the Countenance said to me
0781   Son of the proud ones, do not
0782   pride yourself over[1] your companions and do not say
0783   only I am privileged above all, for it[2] is not from your power
            and might,
0784   but from the power[3] of your father who is in heaven.
0785   But <your father in heaven> you are happy in this
0786   world and it will be good for you in the world to come,
0787   and you are happy and it will be good for you forever and ever
            and ever.
0788   And similarly for all people who hold to it
0789   and say from morning until morning a prayer like yours.
0790
0791   *Section 25 (Paragraph 585)*
0792   R. Ishmael said:
0793   As soon as /I heard/[1] from ŠQDHWYH angel of the
            Countenance,
0794   I stood in all my strength.
0795   and /trembled/[2] and I gave the sanctification
0796   before the king of the world and I said:
0797   Adonai my God, let you be sanctified forever <let you be
            sanctified>.

0798 Let you be exalted over the beasts[3]

0799 and over the chariots of your strength.

0800 Let you be glorified, let you be blessed.

0801 because there is sno one like you.

0802 Let you be sanctified

0803 because there are no works like yours.

0804 For the heaven of heavens recounts your justice

0805 and the awesome tell of your glory.

0806 Seraphim from above and below bow down before you

0807 /because/ you are great and awesome[4]

0808 and there is no ascent and forgetting[45] before the throne of your glory.

0809 Blessed are you Adonai creator of all the creatures in truth.

0810

0811 *Section 26 (Paragraph 586)*

0812 R. Ishmael said:

0813   As soon as R. Nehunya ben Hakana[1]

0814 heard that I stood opposite heaven[2] and detailed off

0815 every angel[3] which is in each and every palace,

0816 he said to me: For what reasons did you detail off the

0817 angels who stand at the gate of the palaces?

0818

0819   I said to him: Not to extoll myself did I do it,

0820 but to praise the king of the world.

0821

0822 R. Ishmael said:

0823   R. Nehunya ben Hakana my teacher said to me:

0824 (The) Torah of /truth/ which Aaron the

0825 Priest[4] acquired for you.[5] It stands by you and there was no pain for you

0826 on account /of this mystery./[6]

0827 But if you wish /to make use of this mystery strengthen your-self/[7]

0828 with five prayers which I say to you.[8]

0829 At that hour he arranged before me five[9] prayers and each and every

0830 prayer is twelve letters[46] from the name of the God,[13]

---

45. The mention of forgetting is reminiscent of the prince of the Torah material and especially section 11.

0831   living and established, the God whose power is
0832   proclaimed and who is sanctified[14] in justice adorned, who sits
0833   on the wide places of the heights.
0834
0835   /R. Ishmael/ said: As soon as /R. Nehunya ben Hakana
0836   my teacher/[11] arranged before me these five[12] prayers,
0837   each day I was praying each and every one with its names,
0838   on the descend and the ascent
0839   and there was relaxation (?) sealed[13] in all my limbs.
0840
0841   *Section 27 (Paragraph 587)*
0842   The first prayer which Z<WPY>L prince of Gehenom[47]
0843   was praying when seeing[1] the Just Ones[52] and
0844   they arranged[2]/[48] Adonai God of Israel /in the/[3] garden of
             Eden[49]
0845   with them and my teacher said to me: He was praying
0846   that prayer which will rescue you[4] from the judgment of
             Gehenom.
0847   And this is the first prayer:[5]
0848   Let you be blessed God, great and mighty,
0849   strong king who is raised in majesty, distinguished in /glory./[6]
0850   You spoke and the world existed.
0851   By the breathe of your lips you established the firmament
0852   and your great name is pure and elevated
0853   over all the ones above and over all the ones below.
0854   Privilege of the earth is your name.
0855   And privilege of the heavens is your name.
0856   And angels stand in your name[7] and Just Ones feel confident
             in your name.[8]
0857   <In> your remembrance flies over all.
0858   And your remembrance is magnified over all living beings.

---

46. While the prayers are described as "twelve letters," they are hymns similar to those in the Akiban section, and contain many more than twelve letters.

47. This character does not appear elsewhere in the text and is not a common figure from the Hekhalot texts.

48. Other manuscripts have letter-clusters here, as part of the name of the divine figure. Perhaps the word *arranged* was picked up from its appearance in the previous section (26) in line 836.

49. According to *III Enoch* 5:1, the divine presence lived in the garden of Eden after the expulsion of Adam.

0859   Blessed is your name alone.

0860   Blessed is your name alone.

0861   Fire which ignites a flaming flame[50]

0862   Z<N >PSP> >Š (fire) >LKLT (consuming) >Š (fire) ZY<M Z<WPH YR>H

0863   ŠRPYM (Seraphim) Z>Ṣ WR (rock) KSYP Ṣ PṢ PM MMŠLT (rulership) >WPNYM (Ophanim)

0864   ḤZQT DLWQH Z<WPH DLWQH DPWSH DBR (word) MḤQQ BHQYH >BṢ BṢ BBṢ

0865   Blessed is your name alone

0866   LBDW Z<WM WDSWM YPṢ <NM ZHYR LṢRŠ ZYWH YWN RM DBWR

0867   BR> DBRY YH YHW YHWY of hosts

0868   Let you be sanctified who created heaven and earth

0869   Your remembrance, all the mighty[9] heavenly companies will praise.

0870   The deeds of your names,[10] from your inhabited world (will be praised?)

0871   Our God, creator of everything,

0872   distinguished in might[13] and beloved in might.

0873   The mighty ones of power confess because they stand before you in truth and justice.

0874   Blessed are you Adonai, majesty of the worlds

0875   and lord of all the rulership.

0876

0877   *Section 28 (Paragraph 588)*

0878   The second prayer:[1]

0879   Let you be sanctified, Adonai God of Israel,[2] heaven and earth.

0880   Lord of lords, distinguished one of distinguished ones

0881   /God of the/ cherubim, rider of the cherubim,

0882   God of hosts, and his ruleship is over the hosts.

0883   God[3] of servants and his name is sanctified by his servants.

0884   He is his name and his name is him.

0885   He is in him and his name is in his name.[4]

0886   Song is his name and his name is song.

0887   Z<WPH Z<P ZW<W ZY< >HSY HWH SYN DMYY YHWH HW> (he) RGŠ BRQ >NY (I) G>H

---

50. This is a good example of the problem with the letters – are these "words" or are they letter clusters?

0888   HW> (he) ḤYL >H >HY >H HW> (he) HW>B ZYD
        >WL DDSDHW RM (high) <L (over) RBW
0889   Zealous, let him be praised, let him be praised zealous,
0890   strength (in) strength,[5] power in power,
0891   might in might, greatness in greatness,
0892   storm in storm, existence in existence,[6]
0893   shadow in shadow, ŠDY will take refuge.
0894   Let you be sanctified, king of the world.
0895   because everything depends on your arm and
0896   all announce praise to your name
0897   because you are lord of the worlds.
0898   There is none like you in all the worlds.
0899   Blessed are you Adonai, the holy one in the chariot,
0900   and rider on cherubim.
0901   *Section 29 (Paragraph 589)*
0902   The third prayer:[1]
0903   Blessed is your name, holy is your name, strong[2]
0904   distinguished over mysteries above and below.
0905   Lord of miracles, lord of mighty acts,
0906   lord of wonders, lord of clarifications
0907   who gives wisdom to the wise
0908   and knowledge to the one acquainted with understanding.
0909   God of Gods, <God of Gods> lord of lords,
0910   the God great, mighty and awesome.
0911   God most high, *creator in his compassion* sitting in highest
        secrecy,
0912   doing wonders and mighty acts and many wonders,
0913   distinguished, strong, awesome and well known.
0914   God, great, mighty over all awesome actions (awesome ones?)
        and mighty deeds.
0915   Adonai one law is his name,[51]
0916   >H *YHHQ* BḤYL ḤBYB ḤQ ḤRZR KR<WTYH MG?S
        >ṬWRYN YQR NŠY> ZH ZH HP
0917   HP RBMṢ YH MWPWM >RPS KY < >H >YH >PWKY
        >PKY ḤY Adonai, God of the world.
0918   You are one and your name is one.

---

51. This is another example of a difficult line, which should not be over-translated. That
is, here again we may have sound clusters.

0919   Lord of all majesty[3] of all the worlds.

0920   Who is like you, living Adonai, my king and my creator?

0921   Who is like your glory, God living and established?

0922   Your glory is full of magnificence and majesty.

0923   Your sanctity is pure and humble.

0924   Therefore[4] mighty ones of heaven extoll you

0925   and the distinguished ones of the earth adorn you

0926   because there is no one like you in heaven or on earth.

0927   Blessed are you Adonai, Lord of every living being.

0928

0929   *Section 30 (Paragraph 590)*

0930   The fourth prayer:[1]

0931   Your name is distinguished on the whole earth and heaven.[2]

0932   You established your throne.

0933   Your dwelling place you set on the tops of the heights,

0934   your carriage you set in the high places.

0935   Your residence (you set) in the clouds of purity.

0935   For your remembrance companies of fire adorn,

0937   for your praise seraphim of fire laud,

0938   The ophanim and the holy beasts stand before you.

0939   And ophanim of majesty and seraphim of flame and the wheels
          of the chariot,

0940   with a raging voice, great and thundering[3]

0941   they say in remembrance in the name,

0942   TWTRWSY Adonai 112[4] times and they say:

0943   ṬṬRSY ṬṬRSYP ṬṬRSY> ṬṬRGY< ṬṬRGYM ṬṬMWPB
          TWṬRKSY ṬṬRYGG ṬRY >BTRY GHṢ GYQQ>

0944   >GH GHYH >PYPBYH B<WR ṬRKSY ṬRYS >KSR
          SṬYṬYY >RWH >BYKH >HYHH >N HN

0945   YHP ṬWḤN ṬYPYYṬY <ṬRSRYH TRPSM ṬYRSYW
          SYṬRPWM

0946   DPYW RDNN >GR HPYWWDDDṢ <S GHS >RSSYH
          PYSP YH HHH YPYPP YQDT> YHṢ P RWṢ Ṣ RHP

0947   DHWP DḤṢ DḤṢB ḤṢB >Š HQ BSQ >BWG BWGBQQ
          YBQK RK YHGYW YHṬṬRSWP ḤPṢ Ṣ

0948   YHGṢ YPWP SPP >RKY ḤWPṢ Y MʔSY <TY <P<WP
          <WP <WPYNP >KYR SBBW YRGH

0949   ṬS GRYZ DLSPSYS YH ṢMṢ ḤṢQṢ ZWYRB >ŠBB YHS
          YHP YHQ QYR

0950 SWPLKPS >>G GBG BZG >GYD DYGRYW >SB>S
      PSPY> ṬṬRYSG

0951 HGYG> HY HWY HW> HW> ḤY YHW> WWY
      HGY> SGY?N NZQ <NRWG >YKR

0952 ṬRPSYSMN HD HWD W>RBH HGG> MHGN>
      HTLTYH KWNS >NGYS WHNBWS MQṬL

0953 HPQS PQS NRWS BHL BRK YPP RGŠT RBB BPT L>
      >BQ PRQ HQQ MRQQ >KKWWK >KSWP

0954 >ḤSD >HG>H >HYG> >HW PTG> <BDTKY ṬKṬWB
      ṬWB ṬBY YHWQ HL YH HP

0955 YHG MBSY< YHWH <S YWGY SYGY WMHGYHW
      YHGR SBRH ŠLT GYD

0956 ŠBY DRWP >YP>WP ><YP<WP >BY HG> YH QRQK
      HW HW WṬRṬSYH YHWH

0957 Holy is your name in your name,[5]

0958 Your name is high and exalted over all the cherubim

0959 Let your name be declared holy in the sanctification.

0960 Let it be magnified in greatness.

0961 Let it be made mighty in might,

0962 and your rulership is until the end of all the generations

0963 because your might is for the eternity of eternities <of
      eternities>.

0964 Blessed are you Adonai, distinguished in power, great in might.

0965

0966   *Section 31 (Paragraph 591)*

0967 The fifth prayer:[1]

0968 Adonai, my God, you became very great;

0969 magnificence and majesty you wore.

0970 And who *KMKK* is like you, distinguished in the heights?

0971 Happy are those who trust in you.

0972 Blessing your name, praising, adoring, extolling, befriending
      your name;

0973 great, mighty and awesome.

0974 Causing to arrive before you blessing, song and chant,

0975 extollation, thanks, and chant, psalm, privilege and truth,

0976 justice, sanctification, purity, and cleansing, and ablution,

0977 shouting, gladness, friendship, faithfulness, kingship, humility

0978 greatness, might, distinguishedness, rejoicing, joy, and happi-
      ness,

0979 /magnificence,/[2] majesty, glory, royal tribute are yours holy God,

0980 high and exalted king,

0981 majestified king, majestic king,[3] distinguished king, majestic king, uplifted king.

0982 ZYRZY>L Ṣ WRṬQ ṬWPGR ṬṬRSP ZBYRY>L BHNYH T<Ṣ Š *<ŠRWW*

0983 >ŠRWY LWW ṬWRṬBW>L HDRYRWM >DRYR*S*

0984 Let your name be blessed forever eternally,

0985 and your kingdom forever and ever,

0986 your dwelling place for eternity,

0987 your throne from generation to generation.

0988 Your eternity is in heaven and on earth,

0989 your rule over the host of[4] the heights and the depths.

0990 And all bring before you song, praise and adoration.

0991 Adonai, your name is more just than all.

0992 You[5] are the eternal rock.

0993

0994 R. Ishmael said:[6]

0995   R. Nehunya ben Hakana said to me:

0996 Everyone who prays this prayer in all his power can catch sight of

0997 the splendor of the presence and

0998 the presence is beloved to him.

0999

1000   *Section 32 (Paragraphs 592-94)*

1001 R. Ishmael said:

1002   My teacher (Akiba) said to me:[1]

1003 I prayed a prayer and caught sight of the presence[52]

1004 and I saw all that they do before the throne of his glory

1005 and this is the prayer:[2]

1006 Blessed are you, Adonai, great is your name in might.

1007 One is your name and there is none like you.

1008 In the heights of heaven you established the heavens, your throne forever.[3]

1009 In wisdom you are distinguished.

1010 In wisdom, intelligence

1011 and in understanding you created your world.

---

52. The phrase *catch sight of the presence* also occurs at the end of the previous section, which may help explain the organization.

1012   In your distinguishedness you created the brilliant cherubim[4]
1013   Silent companies standing before your throne of glory.
1014   You fixed the whole, high and heights.[5]
1015   And established your throne,[6] and adoration, the song of adoration and adornment.
1016   And all the mighty ones and Seraphim[7] who stand before you adore and adorn your name.
1017   And the wheels of the chariot sing song before you.
1018   And you established your throne of glory.[8]
1019   And angels of service who stand and declare holy the holiness of your name
1020   make great your might and say:
1021   Adonai of hosts ŠDY YHW lives forever.
1022   Your kingdom is from one end of the world until the other.
1023   Everything you created in your world recites to your name.
1024   Who is like you?
1025   Great is your name forever, your holiness is forever.
1026   Your might is over all the chariot.
1027   Your distinguishedness is over all[9] the holy beasts
1028   because you live and are established
1029   forever, all of your world.
1030   You are pure and your compassion is interwined[10]
1031   over the brows of kthe beasts for the eternity of eternities.
1032   Beloved and singular are you.
1033   You loved who you (?)[11] in your entire world
1034   and truth and justice are your name.[12]
1035   Your throne is magnificence and majesty,
1036   glory and royal tribute, holiness and purity.
1037   Cleansing and ablution, royal tribute and victory rise before you.
1038   (593) Let you be magnified and declared holy forever,
1039   king, God[12] high and exalted,
1040   because there is none like you in the heavens and on earth,
1041   in the depths and in the sea.[13]
1042   In the heights of Shaked the throne of your glory sings.
1043   And the Aravoth firmament, where your throne dwells..[14]
1044   In them, ones of distinguishedness and powerfulness are complete.
1045   Before you joy and happiness rise up.

1046	The ophanim of majesty and the cherubim of holiness sing song.
1047	/Clouds of/ consolation, the holy beasts proclaim chants.
1048	Their mouths are /hail,/[15] their wings are water
1049	and they bring ZYH ZYHYWN[16] to your name, eternal rock.
1050	Holy, holy holy YWWN YYH YHY YHY *HW* YHW ḤY ŠLMWN YH ḤNYH YHW YH YH.
1051	Holy is your name, your servants are holy.
1052	Adonai One God, high and exalted,
1053	chant and fear fill your throne of glory.
1054	Let you be blessed, you be praised, you be adorned, you be raised,
1055	you be exalted, you be magnified, you be extolled.
1056	you be declared holy, you be majestified, you be loved,
1057	because you established on your throne song, tune, songery,
1058	and praise, adoration and tune, psalm and royal tribute and victory.[17]
1059	And you know the mysteries of above and below, uncovered before you.
1060	And who can[18] speak the song and praise of your great name,
1061	for it is great forever and ever and ever.
1062	Who can recount your chariot?
1063	Forever let you be blessed by all the host /on high/ *let you be blessed,*
1064	let you be made great[19] by the ophanim of majesty,
1065	let you be declared holy by cherubim of holiness,
1066	let you be declared majestic by the chambers of chambers.
1067	let you be adorned by companies of fire,
1068	let you be loved by holy beasts,
1069	let you be praised by the throne of your glory,
1070	who stand before you and sing before you every day
1071	and bring extollation to your name, great, might and awesome,
1072	because there is no one like you in the heavens or on earth.[20]
1073	Blessed are you Adonai, the holy God.
1074	
1075	*Section 33 (Paragraphs 595-596)*
1076	R. Ishmael said:
1077	I said to R. Akiba;

1078   How can one gaze above the Seraphim who stand over the head of

1079   RWZYY Adonai God of Israel?

1080   He said to me:[1] When I ascended to the first palace,

1081   a prayer *and I saw from the first palace* I prayed and I saw from the palace

1082   <to> of the first firmament up to the palace of the seventh firmament

1083   and as soon as I ascended to the seventh palace I recited (the names of) two angels and

1084   I gazed at above the Seraphim and these are them STR HGLYWN.[2]

1085   And as soon as I recited their names,[3]

1086   they came and grabbed me and they said to me:

1087   Human, do not be afraid.

1088   He is the holy king, for he is holy[4] over the throne, high and exalted,

1089   and he is chosen forever and distinguished over the chariot.

1090

1091   At the same time I looked above the Seraphaim who

1092   stand above the head of RWZYY (mystery) Adonai God of Israel

1093   (596) and this is the prayer:

1094   Blessed are you Adonai, one God.

1095   Creator of his world in his [one] name.

1096   Fashioner of all by one word.

1097   In the heights of the heavens you founded your throne.

1098   And your /dwelling place/ you placed in the elevations of the heights.

1099   Your chariot you placed in the upper reaches on high.

1100   Your residence you fixed near the ophanim of majesty.

1101   Companies of fire adorn praises for your remembrance.

1102   Seraphim of fire laud for your praise.[5]

1103   They all carry a small silence,

1104   /and say praise in their palaces./[6]

1105   In awe they walk, in fear they wrap themselves.

1106   Laden with pride to adorn the creator of all.[7]

1107   Covered with eyes on their backs,

1108   their appearances are like the appearance of lightning.

1109   Their splendour is pleasant, wise, sweet[8]

1110   This one in conjunction with that one, they exalt and bring forth.

1111   Exalt and bring forth, pure beasts:[9] Holy, holy, holy.

1112   Angels of services[10] utter before you.

1113   A globe of sun is the host in their mouth.[11]

1114   Their /splendor/ glistens like the brilliance of the firmament.[12]

1115   Their wings are spread out,[13] their hands stretched forth.

1116   In[14] the voice of great waters is the voice of their wings.

1117   Torches of fire they stir up and send out from the globes of their eyes.[15]

1118   In a great noisy voice they sing song before you.

1119   Full of splendor they give forth shining light.

1120   Their splendor glistens.[16]

1121   Pleasant at their going forth

1122   and happy at their comings and glad at their standing.

1123   Their glow is pleasant before the throne of your glory.

1124   In awe /and fear/ they do your desires.

1125   They bring to your name, great, mighty and awesome,

1126   adornment and glory.

1127   And they recite for the recitation of your kingdom[17]

1128   shouting and gladness

1129   because there is none like you,

1130   none like your priests and none like your pious ones.

1131   Nothing like your great name

1132   forever and ever and ever.

1133   Raging at sea and on dry land,

1134   a watcher on land and shaker of it (?)[18]

1135   The whole world shakes from your might,

1136   raising the dead and causing the dead to stand up from smoke.[19]

1137   Your name is great forever,

1138   your name is distinguished forever,

1139   your name is holy forever.

1140   God is one, Adonai is one

1141   YH YH YHW HW> YH ḤY forever

1142   HW YHW is your name forever.[20]

1143 Adonai is your remembrance
1144 from generation to generation.
1145 SRTYK Z<N Y<PY YH MQM> NQS WNQWN <D
      DWD >BG BGBWY HGG HW YH[21]
1146 Forever is your might,
1147 forever is your holiness,[22]
1148 forever in the heavens and on earth.
1149 Therefore let us all call your name,
1150 let us bless your might, let us lift up,
1151 and let us bring extollation before the throne of your glory[23]
1152 because there is none like you in the heavens and on earth.
1153 Blessed are you Adonai, eternal rock.

Notes (Variants)

Section 1 [Scholem] (Paragraph 544 [Schaefer])

1. Lines 5-6:   D 436 reads *I asked R. Akiba a prayer that a man prays, praise of RWZYY;*

      M 22 and O 1531, *I asked R. Akiba a prayer that a man prays and so forth, praise of RWZYY;*

      M 40,   *A question I asked R. Akiba a prayer that a man prays, praise of RYZ.*

2. Line 11:   M 40 and D 436 read, *crown* (KTR) instead of *glory* (KBWD).

3. Line 13:   N 8128   missing part of phrase found in four other manuscripts.

4. Line 15:   All four lack *taught them* (LMDN).

Section 2 (Paragraph 545)

1. Line 23:   All four read *inside* (BTWK) instead of *in all* (BKWL); (N 8128 may have picked up *all* from earlier occurrence in line)

2. Line 25:   M 22 and M 40 have slightly different sequence of dimensions.

Section 3 (Paragraph 546)

1. Line 32:   All four lack *this* (also not found in *III Enoch*).

2. Line 37:   D 436, M 40 and O 1531 read *on it* (LYW), M 22, *before him* (N 8128 may have picked up *before* from the previous line).

3. Line 40:   D 436 and M 40 read *this throne* (KS> ZH);
            M 22,   *before them* (LPNKM);
            N 8128,   KSYH (corruption of *throne* and *this*?)
            O 1531,   missing >.

4. Line 44 (end)-51 are missing in O 1531.

5. Line 47:   N 8128   missing part of phrase found in four others manuscripts.

6. Lines 59-60: Manuscript show slight variants: no version is particularly clear.

Section 4 (Paragraphs 547-49)

1. Lines 65, 68, 75:All four read before line 65: *And what does RWZYY Adonai God of Israel (do)?* also found in *III Enoch*.
    D 436, M 40, R. Ishmael said . . .He said to him . . . Therefore listen to what R. Akiba said to him . . .;
    M 22,   *He said to R. Ishmael . . .He said to him . . . Therefore listen to what R. Akiba said to him*
    . . .
    O 1531,   *R. Ishmael said to me . . . He said to him . . . Therefore listen to what R. Akiba said to him*
    . . .

2. Line 78:   N 8128 reads *HWZ*.

3. Line 80:   O 1531, M 40 and D 436 read *work*

4. Line 89:   D 436 and M 40 lack *holy in heaven,* N 8128 lacks entire phrase.

5. Lines 94-96 lacking in four other manuscripts.

6. Lines 102-104 lacking in four other manuscripts.

7. Lines 108-111 lacking in four other manuscripts.

8. Line 118:   O 1531 reads *compassionate and merciful*

9. *Line 122:*   M 22   *adds in the sea* (BYM).

10. Line 122:   M 40 and D 436 read *on high* (MRWM) instead of
                     water (MYM).

11. Line 132:   D 436 and M 40 read *They sing and they praise and they*
                     sanctify and they bless.

12. Lines 138-39 lacking in four other manuscripts
                     D 436, M 40 read *?* (QSWB), M 22.? (HNWT)
                     instead of *hewn* (HSWB).
                     D 436, M 40 and O 1531 end with line 140 *etc.*
                     M 22 adds several extra lines.

13. Lines 142-143 are the same as in 192.

Section 5 (Paragraphs 550-51)

1. Line 149:   M 40 and D 436 read *before* (LPNY);
                     M 22,   *to praise* (LSBH).

2. Lines 163-64 lacking in all four other manuscripts.

3. Lines 183-84   D 436, M 22 and M 40 have slight variants in phras-
                     ing.
                     O 1531   skips from 170 to *eternally and forever eter-*
                                 nally you will rule forever and forever of holy
                                 forevers.

4. Line 192:   O 1531 reads *You created the heights and the depths by*
                     your word YWY, distinguished in chambers of song.
                     M 22   adds two paragraphs.

Section 6 (Paragraphs 554-55)

1. Line 198:   D 436 and O 1531 read *Ishmael* instead of *Akiba.*
                     D 436 adds *and to ascend* (WL<LWT) before *to catch*
                     sight of

2. Line 200:   All four use infinitive form *to catch sight of*
                     (WLṢ PWT);
                     N 8128,   (MWṢ PWT).

3. Lines 204-29   The numbers vary from manuscript to manuscript.

4. Lines 229-30:   D 436 and M 40 end with *fire.*
                     M 22 reads after *fire; And there is no end to the flames*
                     interspersed between them.

5. Lines 232-83:   All four lack *scatter* in several places.

6. Line 264:   M 22:   ends with *dwelling place of his presence* (same phrase as final line 283)

7. Line 273:   O 1531, M 40 and D 436: *king of kings of kings*

8. Line 276:   O 1531:   adds *on high* (MRWM)

9. Line 279:   N 8128:   (SWRH) (corrupt reading)

10. Line 280:   M 40:   includes *the name of* (ŠM ŠL) as part of divine name (ŠMW>L NHWY)

Section 7 *(Paragraph 556)*

1. Line 288:   M 40 reads *asked* (Š>L).

2. Line 288:   M 40 reads *this mystery*, M 22 phrase unclear.

3. Line 289:   M 22 adds *power of* (GBWRT) before *Torah*.

4. Lines 290-91:   D 436 phrase unclear
M 22 (ḤZR) instead of (HDR) *chamber*.

5. Line 292:   O 1531, M 22, M 40, and D 436, read *chambers* (ḤDRY) instead of *ranks*.

6. Line 292:   M 40 and D 436, read *guard* (ŠMW) instead of *name* (ŠMW).
M 22 lacks *name*.

7. Line 293:   M 22 reads *angels* (ML>KKYM) instead of *in his praise* (M 22 needs word *angels* because does not have *ranks* in previous line).

Section 8 *(Paragraph 557)*

1. Line 301:   D 436 and M 40 read *male* (GBR) for *man* (>DM)

2. Line 302:   All four read *brings* (MGY<). N 8128 (YGY<)

3. Line 302:   All four read BRWKYY i.e. divine name instead of *cherubim* (KRWBY)

4. Line 307:   O 1531, M 22 and D 436 read *will cancel* (YBṬL), M 40 (YKLWL), N 8128 (BṬL).

5. Line 308:   O 1531, M 40 and D 436 read (YNDH) *banish, excommunicate*. M 22, ?(YGRH). N 8128: ? (YṬH).

6. Line 309:   O 1531, *name* becomes part of divine name BŠNYṬ<N TRWGG Adonai. M 22, *name* becomes part of divine name BSNY TYGN. M 40, different divine name NWRWGG. D 436, different divine name T<G TRWNG.

Section 9 (Paragraph 558)

1. Line 319:   All four lack *thus*.

2. Line 324:   All four read *when I ascended to* (BŠ<H KŠ<LYTY).

3. Line 327:   N 8128 spells *holy* with extra (H) at the end, which may have been picked up from *sanctification* in next line.

4. Line 331:   M 40 and D 436, add *the world* (H<LWM) after *created; for the creating* (LHBR>WT) after *commanded*. M 22 lacks *created*.

5. Line 332:   All four add *of service*.

6. Line 334:   O 1531, M 40, and D 436 add *and I shook* (WNR<RTY).

7. Line 335:   O 1531, M 40 and D 436 lack *you*, read *who* instead of *you* in line 336.

8. Line 338:   All four others read *of above* (M>LH) instead of N 8128 (M>LT).

9. Line 341:   All four others read *distinguished* (>DYR) instead of *Lord* (<DWN)

10. Line 343:   O 1531 reads *your work* (Š<MLK) instead of *who stand* (Š<MDYM)

Section 10 (Paragraph 559)

1. Line 351:   O 1531 and M 22 lacks *I asked Akiba*

2. Line 369-370 missing in N 8128.

3. Line 374:   Four others read *beasts* (HYWT) instead of *camps* (HNWT)

4. Line 376:   Four others read *from the foot* (MRGL) instead of N 8128 ? (ZMRGL).

5. Line 378:	N 8128 has (QDWŠTM) which seems to be corrupt version of *holy king, high and exalted* (QDWŠ MLK RM) in four others.

Section 11 (Paragraphs 560-62)

1. Line 387:	M 22 reads *this secret* (RZ ZH) instead of *prince* (SR) *and revealed to him* (WGLH LYW) instead of passive *was revealed* (NGLH); M 40 lacks *of the Torah* (ŠL TWRH).
2. Line 389:	D 436 and O 1531 read *to him* (<LYW) instead of *is revealed to me* (NG<H LY); M 22 lacks *who* (MY SHW<) and has *everyone who is revealed to him*, instead of *is revealed to me*. M 40 reads *everyone who will seek him* (MY SYBQS <LYW).
3. Line 392:	All four read (YTBWL), N 8128 (YTBYL).
4. Line 395:	O 1531 reads *be directed* (WYKWYN).
5. Line 396:	M 40 reads *his name* (SMW) instead of *himself* (<Ṣ MW).
6. Line 399 ff.:	All four vary as to letter manipulations. Same in lines 420-425, 435-438.
7. Line 421:	All four read *above my head* (MR>ŠY).
8. Line 423:	All four read *secrets* (HRZYN), N 8218: ? (HR>YN).
9. Line 424:	N 8218, D 436, M 22, O 1531 read *sink?* YŠTQ<W; M 40 reads ? (YSTQNṬ).
10. Line 442:	All four read *in the order of* (BŠDR) instead of *in secret* (BSTR).
11. Line 451:	All four lack *and earth*.
12. Line 453:	M 22 reads (ḤQYRWT) instead of (ḤQR) (variant spelling of *investigation*. D 436 reads ? (BWNH), *in his heart*. M 40 and O 1531 read *in his heart*.
13. Line 454:	D 436, M 40 and O 1531 adds *it* (>WTW), after

pray, D 436 reads *in his name, and call out his name* instead of *proceed*, adds (BR'Y) after *his name*.

14. Line 455:   All four add *for him* after *make*.

15. Line 455:   All four read *in it* (BH) instead of N 8128 *on the earth*.

16. Line 456:   M 22 reads ? (WYRMZW) instead of *whisper to him* (LW), (WYHRGW >WTW) instead of (WYRGWHW), (variant phrasing, no meaning change) and adds *Ishmael said, the angels* instead of *like angels*.

                 M 40 and O 1531 read *to him* (LW) instead of *to me* (LY).

Section 12 (Paragraph 563)

1. Line 460:   D 436, M 22 and M 40 read *prince* (ŠR).

2. Line 461:   M 40   lacks *who*; M 22 has *requests* (MBKŠ. All four lack *word* in this line, is found instead in line 426 before *one*.

3. Line 462   D 436, M 40, O 1531 lack *If he forgot*
                 M 22   adds after *forgot, one word of it*

4. Line 464:   In all four letter manipulations vary.

Section 13 (Paragraph 564)

1. Line 471:   D 436, M 40 and M 22 read *him*

2. Line 472:   N 8128 reads (RBWD) instead of glory (KBWD)

3. Lines 476-78: M 22   lacks lines 476-8.

4. Line 480:   N 8128   lacks *three*.

5. Line 485:   N 8128   lacks *of wisdom*.

6. Line 486:   M 22   adds *I said to him*.

7. Line 488   N 8128 reads (BDWN) instead of (BKWS), M 40 (LBMS); M 40 lacks *and he drank*; M 22 reads after *cup*, YSTH BYT.

Section 14 (Paragraph 565)

1. Line 499:   M 22   begins *I requested this mystery and.*

2. Line 499: None of the versions are clear.

3. Line 500: M 22   adds *great*. All four variants have *name of*.

4. Line 501: M 22   adds *so that I was agitated, I fell backwards*.

5. Line 503: M 22 reads *son of man, Emptyhead! son of deceiver (?RYMH) and a worm (?TWLY<H), use the great name, take for yourself the orders of the Torah.*

6. Line 506: adds *I stood in all my strength*.

7. Line 509: M 22 reads *40 days in fast and prayed every day*.

8. Line 511: M 22   adds *prayers*.

9. Line 511: N 8128 reads *two words* (letter signifiying *ten* dropped out).

10. Line 512: D 436, M 22 and M 40 read (PRQDS); O 1531, (PDWRM). M 40 skips from *words* (line 510) to angel name.

11. Line 514: D 436 and M 40 read ? (WHŠBY<), O 1531, ? (WHŠBYNW).
M 22 reads after *Countenance, he and seventy angels he sent and they caused to dwell* (WHŠKYNW) *wisdom*

12. Line 516: D 436 and M 40 read (PRWDS); O 1531 (PDWRS); M 22 adds *and to see* (PRWDS).

13. Line 516: M 22 adds *R. Ishmael*.

14. Line 517: All four lack line.

15. Line 518: D 436, M 22 and M 40 read *to him* (cf Note above).

16. Line 518: D 436 and M 40 lack *descend*.

17. Line 519-20: D 436 and M 4 read *He said, he descends with the authority of PNQRS Adonai God destroys him:*
M 22   *To PRWDS angel of the Countenance, descend, if he descends from the authority of PNWRS Adonai God of Israel, I destroy him who uses the great name;*
O 1531   *from the authority, destroys him.*

Section 15 (Paragraphs 566-68

1. Line 529: M 22   adds *in seven seals which R. Ishmael sealed himself*

2. Lines 535-37:   All four

3. Line 543:   D 436 skips from midline 543 to line 556. Others
                      have minor variants in line 543.

4. Line 569:   D 436, M 40, O 1531 read *happy* (ŠMḤ) or *happy*
                      God (ŠMH >L) instead of *your name* (ŠMK)

5. Line 570:   D 436 and M 40 read *great is your name, living in the*
                      might of YH.

6. Line 572-575:   D 436 and M 40 read *I recited three names ZYYP his*
                      name skips to *so that...* (575); M 22 reads *I recited three*
                      names even from his name so that he would not approach
                      me in destruction and when he ascended I recited three letters
                      ZH BY> TYB BY GDW<T >TTYT BYH and I sealed
                      myself with five letters so that no approach me angels with
                      damagers;

                      O 1531   same as D 436 and M 40 but adds *from* (M)
                               before *his name, approach* singular (YG<).
                               In all four, letter manipulations vary.

Section 16 (Paragraph 569)

1. Line 589:   D 436, M 40, and O 1531 read *great* instead of *holy.*

2. Line 596:   O 1531 reads *? BGKYZ* instead of *treasure-buildings*
                      (BGNZY); N 8128 reads *in his garden for* (BGNYW
                      KY).

3. Line 597-98:   D 436, M 40 and O 1531 lack *before you* (LPNYK),
                      minor variations in *because wisdom is before you.*

4. Line 602:   O 1531   adds *holy and* before *great*;
                      M 40   lacks entire line 602;
                      M 22 reads for 601-602: *Your name is forever and your*
                      remembrance is forever, holy is your name;
                      D 436 ends at 602 with an additional *forever.*

Section 17 (Paragraph 570)

1. Line 611:   D 436 lacks entire section 17, having only the phrase
                      friendly to him from line 615.
                      M 22 reads *R. Ishmael said, R. Nehunya ben Hakana*
                      said to me, when <when> . . . . . .;

O 1531 and M 40 read *And again I said to R. Nehunya ben Hakana, when* . . . .

2. Line 612:   N 8128   has the third person plural, not consistent with rest of phrase.

3. Line 614:   All four read *HTPLL* instead of N 8128 *TTPLL*.

4. Line 615:   M 40 and O 1531 end with *to him*;
M 22 ends with *to me* (consistent readings for each frame).

Section 21 (Paragraph 579) [M 22 lacks entire section]

1. Line 715:   M 40 and D 436 read *R. Akiba said, R. Nehunya ben Hakana my teacher said*;

2. Line 715:   M 40 lacks *when* and changes *I caught sight* to *he caught sight* (consistent with frame).

3. Line 716:   D 436 and M 40 read *chamber* (ḤDR) instead of *majesty* (HDR).

4. Line 717:   All three read *distinguished ones* (>DYRY) instead of *majesties* (HDWRY).

5. Line 718:   All three read *fire* (MB<RH) instead of (B<RH)

Section 22 (Paragraph 580) [M 22 lacks entire section]

Section 23 (Paragraph 581) [Angel names vary from text to text]

1. Line 752:   N 8128   has (ŚRY), óthers (ŚR).

2. Line 754:   All three add *sits* (YWŠB).

3. Line 756:   D 436 and M 40 read *your mighty acts* (GBWRTYK);
O 1531   *his mighty acts* (GBWRWTWY).

4. Line 767:   D 436 and M 40 read ? (MDNYM) instead of *heights* (MRWM), and lack *and* (W).

Section 24 (Paragraphs 583-84) [M 22 lacks section entirely]

Paragraph 583
1. Line 771:   All three lack *and* (W).

2. Line 773:   All three read *what* (MH) instead of *what* (KMH)

3. Line 775:   O 1531 reads *that not all* (S>YN KL).

Paragraph 584

1. Line 782:   All three add *all*.

2. Line 783:   All three read *that no* (SL>) instead of *for it is not* (KY
                    L>), reverse *power and might*.

3. Line 784:   All three read *power of the might*;
                    O 1531   lacks *but* (>L>);
                    D 436 and M 40 read *angels* (ML>KYM) instead of
                    father.

Section 25 (Paragraph 585) [M 22 lacks section entirely]

1. Line 793:   Personal ending of verb *last* at end of line on N
                    8128

2. Line 795:   N 8128 reads *?* (ZRQTY);
                    All three *trembled* (ZRZTY).

3. Line 798:   D 436 and M 40 end line *with you* (<MK) and skip
                    line 799.

4. Line 807:   M 40   lacks *you are great and awesome and*.

Section 26 (Paragraph 586)

1. Line 813:   All three add *my teacher* (RBY) (more consistent with
                    other frames).

2. Line 814:   D 436 and M 40 read *on my feet* (<L RGLY) instead
                    of *opposite heaven*.

3. Line 815:   All three read *each and every angel* (KL ML>K
                    WML>K) instead of *every angel* (KL ML>K).

4. Line 825:   D 436 and M 40 lack *Priest*.

5. Line 825:   All three lack *for you* (N 8128 may pick up *you* from
                    next phrase).

6. Line 826:   N 8128 corrupt *you do not have on pain but* reverses *pain
                    and on account of*, lacks *of this mystery*

7. Line 827:   N 8128 reads *this mystery to make use of strength to your-
                    self* (corrupt).

8. Line 828:   D 436 and M 40 lack *which I say to you*;
                O 1531   lacks *to you*.

9. Line 829:   D 436 and M 40 read *before them*; all three lack *five*
                (N 8128 repeats *five* from previous line).

10. Line 832:   D 436 reads *sanctified in the chariots of the heights*, lacks
                line 833; M 40 *sanctified in the chariots*, lacks line 833;
                O 1531 ends with *sanctified*.

11. Line 835:   N 8128   lacks *Ishmael* and *R. Nehunya ben Hakana*
                           my teacher.

12. Line 836:   All three lack *five*.

13. Line 839:   All three lack *seal*.

Section 27 (Paragraph 587)

1. Line 842:   D 436 and M 40 lack *which was praying*.

2. Line 844:   N 8128 reads *and they arranged* (WYSDRW) (may
                have been picked up from 829).
                All three read *And YDHYY* i.e. divine name.

3. Line 844:   N 8128 reads corrupt (D) instead of *in the* (B).

4. Line 846:   All three read *with you* (<MK) (awkward).

5. Line 847:   All three lack *And this is the first prayer*.

6. Line 848:   N 8128 reads (BDBWR) instead of *in glory*
                (BKBWD).

7. Line 856:   All three read *in heaven* (BŠMYM) instead of *in your*
                name (BŠMK).

8. Line 856:   All three reverse *your name* and *your remembrance* (line
                857).

9. Line 869:   All three lack *mighty* (GBWRY).

10. Line 870:   All three read *and* before *from your* (syntax still confus-
                ing).

11. Line 872:   All three read *in greatness* (BGDWLH).

12. Line 875:   All three lack *all*.

Section 28 (Paragraph 588) [M 22 lacks entire section]

1. Line 878:   All three lack line 878.

2. Line 879:   All three lack *Adonai* and *Israel*.

3. Line 883:   M 40 reads ? (>LYW), instead of *God* (>L).

4. Lines 885-87   D 436 reads *like* (K) instead of *in* (B);

    M 40   885: *he is like him and his Name is like his Name*

                    886: *his Name is like his Name.*

    N 8128   *Song* spelled (Ṣ 2WR).

5. Line 890   All three read *eye in eye* (>YN B>YN) instead of *strength* (>Z)

6. Line 893   All three place *existence in existence* earlier, with *zealous* in line 889.

Section 29 (Paragraph 589)

1. Line 902:   All three lack line 902.

2. Lines 903, 904: N 8128 lacks *king*.

3. Line 919:   All three read *distinguished* (>DYR).

4. Line 924:   All three read *over* (>L) instead of *therefore* (>L KN).

Section 30 (Paragraph 590) [M 22 lacks section]

1. Line 930:   All three lack line 930.

2. Line 931:   All three lack *heaven*.

3. Line 940:   All three read *trembling and raging* (R<D WR<Š) instead of *thundering* (RSM).

4. Line 942:   All three read *111* (Y'>);

    D 436   ends section in middle of letter manipulations.

5. Lines 957-958:   M 40 reads *holy is your name high and exalted* (QDWŠ ŠMK BŠM RM WNYŠ>); O 1531 *holy is your name, in the heavens of heavens, high and exalted* (QDWŠ ŠMK BŠMY ŠMYM RM WNYŠ) (clearest reading).

Section 31 (Paragraph 591) [M 22 and D 436 lack section]

1. Line 967:   All three lack line 967.

2. Line 979: N 8128 reads *he* (HW>);

M 40 *musical praise* (RYNH), *magnificence* (HWD);

O 1531 ? (RYṢH), *magnificence* (HWD).

3. Line 981: N 8128 reads (HWDR) for this and the subsequent *majestic*.

4. Line 989: M 40 and O 1531 lack *host (of)* (ṢB>).

5. Line 992: M 40 read *amen* (>MN); O 1531; *said* (>M') instead of *you* (>TH).

6. Line 994: M 40 lacks lines 994-98; O 1531 lacks lines 994-997.

Section 32 (Paragraphs 592-94) [D 436 lacks most of section]

1. Line 1002: M 22 reads *R. Akiba said to me;* O1531, M 22, M 40, lacks line 1002.

2. Line 1005: All three read *And what is the prayer?* (WMH HY> . . .)

3. Line 1008-10 Minor variants in word order, etc.

4. Lines 1012-13: Minor variants in phrasing.

5. Line 1014: M 22 and O 1531 read *earth* (TBL) instead of *whole* (KL).

All three read *height and heights* (G>H WG>WT).

6. Line 1015: All three read *glory* (KBWD) instead of *throne* (KS>).

7. Line 1016: All three read *troops (GDWDYM) instead of mighty ones* (GBWRYM). M 40 lacks *and Seraphim*, O 1531 lacks *and*.

8. Line 1018: M 22 adds *song* (SYRH) before *throne*, M 40 lacks *throne*.

9. Line 1027: All three lack *all* (KL).

10. Line 1030 All three read *make great* (MTGDLYN) instead of *intertwine* (MTGLGLYM) (*make great* more standard for text).

11. Line 1032: M 40 reads *you loved the entire world*, O 1531 *you loved* (ZRḤT) *in the entire world*, question mark inserted in text; M 22, SHBTK MZRḤT.

12. Line 1039:   All three add *holy* after *God.*

13. Line 1041:   All three reverse *in the depths* and *in the sea.*

14. Line 1043:   M 22 reads *because your throne* (ŠKS>K) *you established*; M 40, *in your throne* (ŠBKS>K) *you established*; O 1531, *there your throne you established.*

15. Line 1048:   M 22 reads BDD; M 40 *clear* (BRWR); O 1531, *hail* (BRD).

16. Line 1048:   M 22 reads (ZYH ZYHWWN); M 40 *splendor?* (ZYHYWN); O 1531 (WYH ZYHYWN).

17. Lines 1057-58: Variants in placement of *"and"*; all three lack *tune* in line 1058; D 436 picks up from *praise and adoration.*

18. Line 1060:   D 436 and M 40 skip from *can* to *chariot* in line 1062, add *to praise*; M 22 lacks *speak* (LWMR) and *and* after *song*; O 1531 skips from *can* to *recount*, adds *praise.*

19. Line 1064:   D 436, M 40 and O 1531 read *let you be majestified by the Ophanim of majesty*; M 22 *let you be made great by Ophanim of majesty.*

20. Line 1072:   All four reverse *like you* and *in heaven or on earth.*

Section 33 (Paragraphs 595-96

1. Line 1080:   D 436 and M 40 read *he said to him* (consistent with prior use of 3rd person).

2. Lines 1084-85:   In all four, angel names vary.

3. Line 1085:   All four lack *their names.*

4. Line 1088:   M 436, M 40, and O 1531 lack *holy*;
                    M 22 reads *who sits* instead of *he is holy.*

5. Line 1102:   D 436 and M 40 lack *for your praise*, read *to your name*;
                    M 22   *to adorn*, gloss adds *to the creator* before *serapahim.*

6. Line 1104:   N 8128 reads *praise and they say in* (corrupt word order)

7. Line 1106:   All four lack *of all.*

8. Line 1109:   D 436 and M 22 lacks *wise, sweet*; M 40 reads ?

(QYMM) instead of *splendor* (ZYMM) and ? (HYBM) instead of *wise*, lacks *sweet*.

9. Line 1111: D 436, M 22 and O 1531 lack *bring forth*;
M 40 lacks *in conjunction with . . . bring forth*.

10. Line 1112: D 436 and M 40 read *of Shaddai* (ŠDY) instead of *of service* (ŠRT).

11. Line 1113: This phrase is unclear in all versions:
D 436 and M 40 *sinks between them* (ṬB< BYNYHM); M 22 *sinks their faces* (ṬB< PNYHM); O 1531 *flows their faces* (NWB< PNYHM); N 8128, *host in their mouth* (Ṣ B< BPYHM).

12. Line 1114: N 8128 reads ? (<YWM) for *splendor* (ZYWM).

13. Line 1115: M 436 and M 40 read (PRWDWT),
M 22 and O 1531 (PRYŠWT) for both *spread out* and *stretched forth*. N 8128 *spread out* (PŠRWT).

14. Line 1116: O 1531 reads *like the voice* (KQWL) (clearest reading).

15. Line 1117: D 436 and M 40 skips from *torches of fire* to *happy* in line 1121, and then to line 1123;
M 22 reads ? (HS<YN) instead of *send out* (YWS<YM).

16. Line 1122: M 22 and O 1531 lack *glistens*

17. Line 1127: Others construe line 1126 with line 1127, lacking *and* in line 1127.

18. Line 1134: Versions vary, none very clear.

19. Line 1136: M 436, M 40, O 1531 read *from the dust*, M 22 *wakes the dead from their sleep*.

20. Lines 1141-42: In all four, letter manipulations vary.

21. Line 1145: In all four, letter manipulations vary.

22. Line 1148: D 436, M 22, O 1531, M 40 add after 1147 *forever is your kingdom*.

23. Line 1151: Minor variations in all versions:
M 40, D 436 lack *extollation* and *throne*; O 1531 lacks *throne*; M 22 reads *for your holiness extollations* instead of *and let us bring extollation*.

CHAPTER FOUR

The Patterns and Poetics of Ascent: Employing the Name

The bewildering and dense arrangement of *Maaseh Merkabah* begins to unfold for us as we return to the text armed with some understanding of the linguistic ideology discussed in the second chapter. With the help of Jakobson and Silverstein, we will shift from a focus on language as semantics to the functions of poetic language, with its multiple types of efficacy. Our search will focus on poetic tropes, glossing relations, deviations from standard usage, and sound symbolism. Our goal will be to explain "performativity" of a non-semantically based type; i.e., the role of "magical" language.

The text consists of two main textual forms, hymns and the reported-speech introductions to these hymns. Each type of material incorporates the linguistic ideology in a different manner.[1] The hymns, which we will consider before turning to the reported-speech frames, develop a limited set of images including descriptions of the deity as creator, the heavenly chorus, and actions of praising. Our goal is to find the manner in which they not only talk about, or hint at, the transformation of ascent but also establish "copies" of these transformations.

As noted by Tambiah, a major scholar of ritual whose work will be discussed in the last chapter, central rituals often "enact and incarnate cosmological conceptions" (1979, 121). The enacting of cosmological conceptions in *Maaseh Merkabah* is most obvious in the enumerations, which are extreme examples of foregrounding or emphasis on arrangements with multiple repetitions of the exact same phrases. These enumerations (sections 3, 6, 9, and 10) contain numerical listings of the heavens, the occupants of the heavens, or aspects of its physical layout. These compositions repeat entire lines with only minor variations, such as increasingly large numbers. The patterns reflect a multilayered heaven; the description of the first layer sets a precedent to be followed in all subsequent layers but also to be subsumed in a hierarchy. Numerical increases, literally subsuming each previous layer, are a simple way of outlining this hierarchy; increasing levels of purification is another (section 9).

In all these compositions, each level establishes a precedent for the next, a model for the elements found in the next higher level. Each level mirrors and forms a microcosm of the next. A second dimension is added because all levels are not exactly identical. Instead, there is an asymmetry of transformation, with the semblance of hierarchy adding perforce a directionality to the layers. The enumerations connect the arrival at each level with a specific example of a speech act: "When I arrived in the sixth heaven I said the sanctification." The text repeats its message over and over – saying "does" something and the speaker ascends with each utterance.

The enumeration in section 6 (lines 204-72) contrasts a static and a dynamic recitation of the heavens. The first recitation narrates the increasing numbers of fiery chariots and of flames, making a double listing of numbers. Because of the immense numbers involved, it is as if infinities were stacked on infinities, demonstrating, for example, the relation of 2-4-6-8 on a cosmic scale. In the second listing, the chariots perform acts of praise, reciting condensed and formulaic phrases of adoration similar to those found throughout the hymns. The repetition of the praise literally moves the flames from one level to the next, providing the verbal fuel.

These enumerations represent both diagrammatic icons of the heavens and models of ascent through them. These icons of heaven provide a model of the similarity of levels, and of their hierarchical status. The heavens are not simply described, they are ascended through. Each one must be negotiated in order to reach the next. At each step the description of the layer creates the context for recitation of the praise, as in "When I ascended to the sixth palace I said" and "Flames . . . gather together toward the second palace and say." Any two lines of the dynamic ascent, as the flames form and re-form, is itself a mini-ascent, a complete transformation achieved by a short praise formula. When these are piled on top of each other, they form one large ascent, giving the text its prismatic quality. The most complex acts of praise are possible because the context, all prior layers, have already been invoked and traversed. For example, we know that when Akiba said the sanctification, he was already at the sixth palace. Recitation of the sanctification, thereby, indexes the speaker as having arrived on that level.

The enumeration in section 10 ends with a particularly interesting reference to declaring the Name holy "there." *There* is highly context-dependent; the location of *there* is discernible in term of – and only in terms of – the structure of the distances explicated in the enumeration. This location is connected with declaring the Name, which brings us back to the issue of the native ideology about the divine Name.

God's name, like other words he utters, is part of his special language competence, distinct from human competence. The divine Name qualifies as "divine language" in a double sense. It is the name of the diety and thus divine and, at the same time, the name was spoken BY the deity, thus becoming an example – indeed, the most important token – of divine speech. This double divinity underlies the ritual use of the Name. The rabbinic interpretation of the Genesis creation story[2] incorporates a performative ideology distinct from that which the Biblical version seems to represent. According to Genesis, God said, "Let there by light." Not only does this encode a proposition, but the specific deed that results is determined by the reference and predication of the proposition. Uttering the word *light*, light is created.

$$\text{Let there be light} \rightarrow \text{light}$$

$$\text{word} \rightarrow \text{deed}$$

In each act of creation, words uttered in divine speech referred to the items created. God does not speak in distinct performatives, for reference itself is performative, with each word translating into the corresponding deed. All these acts are introduced by the verb *said* for in God's creative speech as depicted in Genesis, the deed is determined simply by reference. To state now that God spoke his Name when he created the world alters the story completely and shifts the underlying notion of the perceived efficacy of God's speech. This new theory, for example, is no longer based on the reference and predication of words uttered by the deity. By stating that the creative word spoken by the deity was his Name, the pragmatics of divine speech have now been located in a specific meaningful unit; that is, the divine Name. The simple relation between the utterance of *light* and the creation of light is gone. The primordial act of creation is no longer the primordial reference; instead it is an act of naming.

The explicit content of the words God spoke, as it were, have been separated from the mode, or implication, of that speech. Divine language is the uttering of divine Names, and the creative word no longer refers to the deed it brings about.

$$\text{"name"} \rightarrow \text{light}$$

$$\text{word} \rightarrow \text{deed}$$

A linguistic concept is introduced here, the concept of the proper name. God's Name, as with many proper names, has no fixed sense, if his utterance has any basis in the semantics of Hebrew.[3] Instead, it has only reference. When he speaks his Name, it does not refer to the deeds it effects but instead to himself.

Genesis creation story	*Maaseh Merkabah*
"Let there be light" → light	"name" → light
refers to	effects
word → deed	word → deed
effects	refers to

God's words are deeds, according to this interpretation, because they refer to him, and hence to his power. Powerful language is now comprised of those words that refer to, or presupposingly index, the source of divine power, the deity. Complete identification of word with deed has been replaced by a system of reference to, as it were, the power behind the throne. Yet, because it is God's own Name, the pragmatics of God's speech have been preserved. Only divine Names carry divine efficacy.

This altered theory of the deity's speech places the divine Names at the center of the ritual language system. While not everyone can say "let there be light" and create light, it is possible to appropriate and teach the powerful goal-directed use of divine language when it consists of God's Name. The language of creation, the paradigmatic creative language, is not the language of reference, except in so far as it reflects back on the divine speaker. Instead, the "content" of powerful speech explains its power, for that speech is the closest representation of power, being literally the name of that power. A proper name is perceived to have a special relation to the person named, as if the name were in some respect that person. Making the name the creative word par excellence "washes out" reference so that divine efficacy is separated from specific application. The model of divine speech can be transmitted to other creative goals; the "performativity" can now be directed to new applications.

The rabbinic reworking of the creative language from Genesis is incorporated into the hymnic compositions by the variety of poetic word-patternings employed.[4] The poetic patterns include strings of words with no syntactic patterning more complex than *and*, extended noun constructs, reversible phrases (*X* is *Y*, *Y* is *X*), explicit equations with the Name, layering a word or a phrase by repeating it throughout a hymn, layering a syntactic pattern with exact repetition or with variations, specially marked openings and closings, and "nonsense" words. We will look briefly at each of these devices.

Sometimes words are simply strung together with no syntax more complex than an occasional *and*.[5] As with the famous heavenly chorus "holy, holy, holy" (Isaiah 6:3), here, too, the words are words of praise. Each word describes the very action the speaker is engaged in, i.e., praise, bless, etc. The person who utters the hymn effects praise of the deity by talking directly about the process of praise. With the recitation of each word, the action encoded in the word is acted out; to talk about is to do.

In addition, the repetition of such praise words creates, quite literally, a chorus of "praises." Modeled on the paradigmatic "holy, holy, holy" the cumulative effect of the strings of words is an exact replica of the repeated praises of the heavenly chorus.[6] At the same time, the sounds are icons of the sounds of the heavenly chorus. The sounds are the basic elements out of which praise is built and copying the heavenly chorus is learning to copy their sounds.[7]

Piling up to words also occurs in the extended noun phrases, such as king of kings of kings.[8] These extended noun constructs are not normally used in speech. The form has been extended beyond the sense limit; for while we can imagine who a king of kings is, a king of kings of kings is a more obscure, if grander, image.[9] These constructs are also icons of the many layers found throughout the text, mirroring the heavens. This extension of the once common noun-construct, with its new play on meaning, is seemingly infinite, as are the heavens.

Yet another way of piling up words is reversible phrases such as

> He is his Name and his Name is him
> He is in him and his Name is in his Name.
> Song is his Name and his Name is song. (28:884-86)

This form is then shortened to reversible phrases that simply "rotate" the noun around a preposition as "eye in eye, power in power, might in might (890)."[10]. These reversible phrases have the same function as the more explicit equations with Name (Name = X) and highlight other equations, some of which are built up less obviously in the extensive parallelism. The special dimension of this form is that the reversal of the phrase literally effects the transformation. The place of "his Name" is now taken by "his song" and that of "his song" by "his Name." The transformation of language, or word, into "his Name" has been carried out on the plane of language. His Name has become his song, and his song has become his Name. His song, equated with his Name, functions in the same manner.

Even as small and seemingly simple a form as this can be analyzed on many levels. The content is self-reflective; to say the words *his song* is to sing God's song. Sound symbolism again is at work; as another icon of heavenly praise, the choice of the word *song* emphasizes sounds and rhythm as much as semantic content.[11]

Other words are transformed into "Name" by explicit equation with name.[12] The import of these equations is not the juxtaposition of objects but the comparison of types of words.[13] Guided by our preliminary conclusions about the Name and its efficacy, we now find that the thrust of these equations is to extend the performative force of the Name to other words. All words equated with the Name entail the same performativity.[14]

$$\text{``Name''} \quad = \quad \text{``word } X\text{''}$$

$$\text{effective word} \qquad\qquad \text{effective word}$$

These equations create a new language in which each word is powerful because it is another of the many Names of the deity.[15]

A selection of words are woven throughout the text with the constant reuse of vocabulary adding to the dilution of the semantic meaning of words.[16] Similarly, the repetition of entire phrases adds to the density of the text and further blurs semantic meanings.[17] Repeated phrases often occur directly before "nonsense" syllables, forming a transition to the densest lines of all. More common than the direct repetition of words and phrases is the weaving together of phrases that are slight variations of each other. The creativity of use involves finding yet another way to layer and alter short syntactic phrases.[18]

The multiple parallels then establish even more equations with Name. Where the number of lexical and syntactic parallels is the densest, the greatest number of juxtapositions have been created. Where the greatest number of comparisons and contrasts are made, the text is maximally ambiguous. It is no longer clear which strand relates to which other, as both words and patterns create links between disparate lines of the text. These structural equivalents, when the Name in its various forms is added, create new definitions of the Name. The density of these network of parallels results in almost every word and phrase being a semantic equivalent of the divine Name. By the inductive extrapolation underlying this, a theory can be discerned in which the Name contains the effective content of every word and phrase in the language. It is pure creation and out of it pours the whole universe of words.

The systematic violation of normal language use, that is, phrases and other linguistic combinations that are not predicable according to ordinary rules of language, is found throughout the text. Every linguistic level is not necessarily integrated into the next higher level; this constitutes the first indication that there is violation of the norm. Phrases often are not used to build sentences, words often are not used to make a standard sentence, but instead are used in a variety of unusual phrases, reflecting the poetic diction of the compositions. Letters are not used to build standard words. These poetic forms are then interspersed among the more standard usages, drawing attention to the forms themselves, their mysteries, and their contributions to the meaning of the text, but also, by juxtaposition, casting a shade of new meaning over the whole.

Moreover, even the repetition of a standard form contributes a new meaning. The repetition of "Blessed is your Name alone" signals that the message has not been delivered in one recitation. Therefore, the larger patterns of composition themselves become deviations from standard usage, through the presence in them of these poetic forms. The nonstandard poetic forms are used to manipulate each linguistic level, so that the level can be integrated into and made use of according to the implicit theory of "performativity." Each pattern, in more or less explicit ways, establishes semantic equivalents for God's Name. Some equations are in the form of definitions of metapragmatic equations (X is your name) as though the Name had a sense or semantic content. The other poetic forms make this same claim, creating the Name substitutes, transferring to substitutes the semantics (reference to the deity) and the pragmatic capacity.

The most striking deviation from normal usage is the frequent occurrence of "nonsense" words. Often labeled *voces magicae*, these words have presented great difficulties in interpretation. They are the symbol par excellence of magical language and its lack of semantic value, and, thus, do not even warrant analysis or explanation. In this text, however, the appearance of the nonsense words is a logical extension of the manipulation of each level of language down to the level of sound. If, according to the special understanding of divine speech, words equal deeds, then even the sound of the words can fill the same function. Sounds have the same efficacy as the words they form. This is an extreme extension of "performativity," in which sounds are elevated to the level of effective units. The sounds are equivalent to words, not as means of conveying semantic value but as directly effective agents.

The destruction of linguistic levels extends to the formation of words. Since the "nonsense" words are made up of letters from the Name, they have the same efficacy as the Name. These words consist entirely of sound, having no recognizable semantic value. Instead, they have the force of, or in a performative view, the "meaning" of, the Name as the creative word. They also refer to the deity. These words highlight the letterness of words and symbolize their inward elaboration. The divine Name also consists of sounds; in creating the world God spoke a series of sounds. This is especially true in *Maaseh Merkabah*'s interpretation, for the deity did not use referential speech. That is, he did not say, "Let there be light." The patterning of sounds makes the reader maximally aware of this nonreferential speech, for sound clusters draw attention to the sounds that compose them. God's Name is presented in terms of its basic constituents. Since performative integrity has descended to the level of pure sound, when these sounds are then used to make "words" or, rather, are arranged in wordshapes, they create especially effective words. In these special words, all the sounds carry the performative value of other performative units, for they too re-create the Name that empowers.

In standard usage, phonemes are employed only to distinguish among words. The phonemes themselves have no direct functionality. Sapir (1925), for example, distinguishes between the sound *wh* used in the word *wheel* and the sound *wh* used to blow out a candle. In the second instance, the sound has a direct function or effect. In this text, such a role is allocated to all phonemes; using the sounds becomes a functional act. The duality of patterning (phoneme/morpheme) of language is destroyed at every instance, and all linguistic elements contain the same force, an inherently pragmatic component.

Since the deity spoke sound and not sense when he created the world, and the text wishes to copy this "sound," the most effective device for emphasis on sounds is to use such "semantically-depleted" words.[19] God's Name is presented over and over, now in terms of the sounds. The words themselves become more like letters, for all letters used carry divine status. These letters are a separate divine language; if words became deeds when spoken by the deity, here sounds equal deeds. The power of speaking is heightened by each and every sound, creating the ultimate in divine language, indeed, inventing "magical" language. The dual patterning by which words are made up of sounds and also convey meaning is destroyed. The distinction between word and sound disappears. The systematic destruction of every level of normal language use has been completed, and the entire text has become a remembrance of the Name. This remembrance is the same as the speaking of the very sounds of the Name.

Thus the ascent hymns are patchworks, composed of praise, divine attributes, and details about the heavenly chorus. The litany of angels who speak the divine Name and songs of the upper world provide a model of divine praise that is reproduced by the individual who ascends. In the enumerations, layerings of repeated phrases are visible immediately as diagrammatic icons of the heavens. The reader climbs from heaven to heaven, as each layer is brought into contact with the next, thereby permitting ascent. Heaven and earth are juxtaposed in the hymns, enabling the reader to negotiate the "staircases" created. The one who recites these hymns becomes part of the heavenly chorus, collapsing the distance between the heaven and earth. The Name, introduced in a myriad of forms including sounds, empowers the whole text.

If the primary speech act is using the Name, the formulas establish cycles of speech acts. They begin with a summation of God's creative activity, such as "You are the living and established God/You created heaven and earth" (lines 335-36). The creation through speech of the heavenly realm brings into existence the heavenly chorus, the second entity after the deity to make use of the Name. The principal activity of this group is to bring praises to the deity. They also teach the lower world to make use of the Name and to praise the deity. The individual taught by a heavenly being then forms an earthly chorus, which becomes indistinguishable from the heavenly chorus. The formulas and frames trace the passing down of the Name, giving instances of Name-use on each of the levels: by God, by heavenly creatures, and finally by the rabbis.

Due to the studied ambiguity of the formulas, it is sometimes impossible to tell which level actually is doing the praising. One line of praise attributed to the heavenly chorus is followed by another line of praise as reports of praise alternate with direct praise, so the distinction is blurred within the formulas. In addition, because the praise is actually recited by the outermost speaker, it becomes simultaneously the behavior of several "choruses."

The hymns are each presented as the content of past dialogues. The dialogic introductions vary as to their presentation; sometimes a formula is presented as a report of a report and sometimes just as a report. What is the purpose of these elaborate reported speech introductions? Reported-speech frames influence the reading of the utterances they frame. Each frame is a second context, articulating to varying degrees attitudes toward and understandings of the utterance. The use, for example, of the verb *promise* to frame an utterance conveys not only the words spoken but also the reporter's attitude toward them and their possible consequences or entailments.[20] In addition, in reported speech, the words spoken and the context of utterance become themselves the subjects of the frame.[21]

Analysis of the reported-speech forms in *Maaseh Merkabah* shows that the actions of praise become themselves the subject of investigation because, literally, praise is talked about. Praise is both an action and a theme of the text, a theme of the reported speech. One individual may enact an instance of praise, and that action will then become the subject of discussion by the next speaker. New contexts are created each time a new speaker reports the words of another, and the formulas are studied in the switch from speaker to speaker.

As reported speech, the text contains interpretations of the role of the formulas; each section describes situations in which the formulas are put to work. The same question we ask – what do the speakers think they are doing by talking this way? – is not only instantiated in the formulas but addressed in the frames as well. The frames, like the formulas, consist of a narrow selection of patterns, employed with the same kind of asymetric parallelism and expansion found in the hymns. The very choice of reported speech as the main pattern for the frames mirrors the verbal core of the ritual and provides a guide for interpreting both the text and the rite. The formulas exist in the text only as speech, and this aspect of their form is inseparable from their function. According to this theory in "He said X," the reader also speaks X and assimilates the performative force of X. There is no duality of patterning; mention is use. The patterning of the frames as reported speech results in their use as speech, in their function as devices to achieve certain goals. The standard form includes the presentation of an outer narrative that introduces the speaker who initiates the reader, followed by reports of a dialogue in which the primary speaker learns or divulges secrets of ascent.

The reported-speech frames also contribute to the ascent text by providing the verbs that activate the ascent process, by guaranteeing the efficacy of the formulas, and by creating the chains of transmission that make the text truly didactic. The verbs in the frames occur in sequences that closely connect a limited number of actions, moving repeatedly from "saying" to "seeing". These same phrases, by stressing that the formulas led from saying to seeing in the past, serve to reinforce the success of each recitation. The frames also set forth the elements necessary for the formulas to be used appropriately and with the desired result, as for example the listing of a pure heart and the proper formula in section 1. In turn, the chain of transmission created in the levels of reported speech and speakers conveys the efficacy of the formulas to the last individual indexed by the chain, namely, the reader.

If we examine one of the more complex frames, as for example the frame in section 1, we find that the speech acts are nested one inside the next, making each one a subpart of the previous one.[22]. The arrangement of the frames transports the formula from speaker to speaker: X said that Y said that Z said. The layering relations are created not as in the hymns by the repetition of words and phrases but by the verbs of speaking that tie one participant to the next, directing questions and answers.

A careful reading of the first frame reveals that it is not a dialogue but a report of a now-past dialogue. The opening "Ishmael said" has no addressee; he is not talking to Akiba but instead is reporting what they said. However, the apparent dialogic situation of the very first frame is impressed upon the reader. He reads the section as if Akiba and Ishmael were having a discussion instead of Ishmael reporting a previous conversation with Akiba. The reader then reads the "enclosed remainder" of the text as if it were direct dialogue.

The patterns of interaction extracted from the frames replicate the teacher-student chains mentioned in section 1 (God → Moses → Israel): in this case, however, each frame is an instance and not merely a description of that relationship. All these teaching sessions are occurrences from the past; each question-answer repeats the basic revelation pattern (deity to Moses) but shifts from a deity-human plane, with one rabbi instructing another.

The specific forms of the frames and their variations of reported speech enable the reader to see the formulas "in action." Because the text presents actual instances of use, the didactic potential of the text is enhanced, for the form of the text, speech, is also the subject of the text. Grasping the impact of the frames is therefore one way of learning the text's message. In addition, the device of reported speech, when combined with the native understanding of effective language, results in a didactic text that conveys not only knowledge about, but also experience of, ascent for the reader/user.

The use of reported speech enables the characters to fully describe the contexts of use. The speakers make explicit not only the saying → seeing connection but also the contextual elements that must be present for the saying → seeing to work. In the process of presentation inherent in the dialogue – the What did you do? – participants tell each other, and thereby the readers, how they used the formulas. The text reads most like a manual in these frames, which discuss the "how-to" of ascent. In this case, however, they do not tell the user in the form of impersonal instructions. Each bit of information or instruction is conveyed by means of instantiation, for the speaker, after describing "when I said . . . I saw," then gives an instance of that kind of behavior.

All of the elements needed to activate the process are outlined in the frames. Akiba states that two things are needed, a pure heart and the proper formula.[23] The frames describes the requirements and then the formula instantiates them. After the recitation of the formula, Akiba did indeed "see." The extremely limited contextual elements reinforce the "automatic" effectiveness of the prayers.

The efficacy is established for the original recitation of each formula. It is then established for each repetition by the theory of language implicit in the text. If the formulas were indeed successful on some previous occasion, and only the pure heart of the reciter is needed, words will equal deeds in all of the subsequent recitations even as what we would call reported speech. In linguistic terms, the contexts created lack external grounding. The frames at no point refer to or index any external world beyond that established by the reported-speech situations. These situations are self-contained worlds, which make the text more easily applicable for the reader and therefore that much more useful as a didactic text. The text strives to set up the most "ahistorical" setting possible.

The frame describes a previous ascent and at the same time delineates the teacher-student relationship by which this success can be repeated. The formula that "a man" is told to say, is spoken by the teacher, Akiba. The frames establish the paradigm for teaching: the process of ascent is learned by asking, followed by reporting of a successful ascent. A chain of transmission extends not just between two people but level upon level. The revelations are brought directly into a teaching situation by the question and answer mode of discourse in the frame. This teacher-student relationship mirrors the many chains of revelation outlined throughout the text. In the very first section Moses learns from the deity and each teacher repeats knowledge derived from that encounter.

The device of reported speech enables the participants in the text to become the latest examples of the link in the chain. The frames moves the reader into the chain, again by exploiting the possibilities of reported speech. While the text seems to be a dialogue, it, as noted, is not. Ishmael is not directly speaking to Akiba; he is reporting a conversation he had on some unspecified occasion. The other half of the outermost dialogue is not Akiba, but the reader. The reader, as implied hearer, completes the chain, automatically being placed in the same relation to Ishmael as Ishmael was to Akiba. Ishmael has abrogated all of Akiba's success to himself, and he now functions as the instructor. He teaches the reader everything that he learned from Akiba. By reading the text, with its present mode of arrangement, it is impossible for the reader not to be placed in that position; by the very reading of the text he becomes the receptive (student) half of the dialogue and his copresence is indexed. The questions to ask are both generated and answered for him. He is corrected just as Ishmael is if he misses any points about ascent. As Ishmael states, the very hearing of the text leads to illumination.

In addition, in several places the text is phrased in the most general terms possible. Thus, the first section states that "a man" says the prayer.[24]

Variation in the explicitness of the frames serves the same purpose. Once the frame is established and then violated in the next section, as in the shift from the first to the second section, the reader is "jumped into" the dialogue. The reader becomes an overhearer of deeper and deeper parts of the dialogue and is drawn into the discussion.

The problem of teaching ascent involves the teaching of the exact replication of the proper formula. The primary didactic model will be talking, for the basic issue to be taught is exactly correct modes of speaking. The formulas can be taught only in their exact replications, for to hint at the general content of the verbal compositions would not answer Ishmael's question.

The frame is a formal equivalent to being able to speak only substitutes for the Name, an attempt to mitigate charges of blasphemy. For even if the speakers do not use God's Name directly, they are still using the deity's mode of speech and thus seeming to blaspheme. Efficacious speech belongs to the deity alone. Due, however, to the arrangements of these complex frames, no individual rabbi ever directly states a formula. These rabbis only are repeating formulas that someone used on a previous occasion. The frame creates other, now-distant situations as origins for the formulas.

The elaborate attempts of the reported speech to distance the reporter from the words of the formulas ultimately fail, defeated both by elements of the frame itself and by the formulas as well. Once each formula is begun, it is repeated in its entirety. The formula is not hinted at or partially described. Each word of the formula is reported creating an exact replica of the successful ascent. If there were any differences between the repetition of the formula and the original use, its efficacy would be negated. Or, if any requirement external to the text were listed, the recitation of the formulas would be unsuccessful. However, in *Maaseh Merkabah*, even the report of a report of praise is exactly the same as its use. Being an icon of the successful praise, it has the same efficacy. Each formula is close to the original utterance; that is, it cannot be distinguished from the original, particularly if the reader's heart is pure. Since the frame states that only a pure heart and the prayer are needed, the presentation of that prayer is immediately effective. If the rabbis attempt to be only reporting, they fail.

The ultimate reason why the frames are a poetic device is the very theory of language contained in the prayers it introduces. These formulas are self-operational, founded on a theory of language according to which words do not simply refer to objects. These words cannot be mentioned without their use and they cannot be handed down as empty words. They do not exist separate from their pragmatic force. Thus, the very notion of quoting – i.e., merely "mentioning" someone else's actual "use" – is impossible. If in Scriptures quoting would have undercut the pronouncement by human beings of God's words, here the opposite issue is the problem – here they strive to adapt the divine modes of speech for human use in ritual.

As reported speech then, the entire text is a contradiction, words cannot be quoted no matter how complex the quoting chain is. Quoting is using, and the one who "mentions" ends up in the seventh heaven just as does the one who "uses."[25] In the shift between the frame and the formulas, the criteria for successful ascent are delineated and then instantiated, the paradigm created and then automatically put to use. The arrangement is the message, for the arrangement is this transformation.[26]

Maaseh Merkabah, thus, has solved the problem of how to teach religious experiences. The importance of teaching these rites is counterbalanced by the problem that the process inherently encounters. How can one teach something that has to be experienced? *Maaseh Merkabah* solves this problem about ascent through the experience of ascent. It establishes the paradigm of a successful ascent, and then collapses every recitation of ascent into the previous successful ascent. Each time a formula is repeated, or reported, it is repeated in the exact form that it was said in an earlier ascent. Each teaching of ascent is merely the reciting of the required prerequisites (formula) of the previous successful ascent, so that the teaching actually is that ascent as well. Akiba's ascent is now the reader's ascent, reported in a system that knows no mere ineffective reporting of effective language forms.

The text is truly didactic because this efficacy is then conveyed to the implied hearer. The reader is embedded into the text in the studied ambiguity of the frame, as it shifts from section to section. The chain of revelation that leads back to Moses and to the deity is brought down to Akiba and then out of the text to the user. The reader cannot avoid this, for as soon as he starts to read he becomes the next link in the chain.

The frames and the formulas do not stand alone nor do they work in isolation. Transition from frame to formula is smoothed by many factors; the framing so closely mirrors the activities described in the formulas that the text moves easily from speaking level to speaking level.

Once ascent through speech is accepted as the overall goal of *Maaseh*

Merkabah, a review of the patterns both in the embedded formulas and in the reported speech frames will account for the particular construction of this text. Details of the parallelistic compositions and the reported-speech frames all contribute to the efficacy of the text as a ritual document and to the usefulness of the text as a teaching device. Every level of language is manipulated in order to present the dynamics of speech and the role of speech in ascent.

These manipulations are motivated by the interpretation of the creation story found in *Maaseh Merkabah*. The dramatic speech of the deity, which summons the cosmic elements into existence, can easily be read as providing a model for speech that does not simply represent but enacts. The system found in *Maaseh Merkabah* similarly employs the word to not merely refer to objects. Unlike the Genesis story, however, the conception of divine speech consists of the Names of the deity.

The two sources in the text have slightly different interpretations of this theory.[27] They both posit a central speech act of praise and use of the divine name that copies a heavenly model. In the Nehunyan source, however, distinct used of the divine Name have been articulated, as seen by the different verbs that define and delineate these actions. They are all subcategories of uttering the Name, the more unific speech act found in the Akiban source. Each incorporates the power of the Name in a different manner. "Recite" (ZKR) is speaking the Name in order to gain wisdom by summoning angels. "Detail off" (PRŠV) is uttering of entire lists of Names or spelling out letters of the Name. "Sealing" (ḤTM) is the speaking of Names as a protective device. The pragmatic component of Name enables these articulated usages to develop.

As it now stands, the text is the result of placing the reported speech frames in front of the formulas. The density of the text stems from the competing modes of organization. Because of the frames, the text is a series of nested speech situations, one inside the next. At the same time, the text builds upward in layers of enumerations and formulas. The two formal arrangements also have conflicting time frames. The reported speech frames try to establish specific, seemingly distant origins for the formulas. The rabbis pretend to be reporting formulas in terms of past events: "When I said . . . I saw." At the same time, the formulas are actually being recited by the outermost speaker in the frame. The primary situation in which a formula was supposedly uttered is not the ultimate situation of utterance, despite the claims of the outermost speaker, for Ishmael is telling the entire text.

Sometimes more than one "ascent" is completed in each formula, because any correct utterance of the Name constitutes a mini or condensed version of the much more complex speech event of the entire text. Thus, the text is like a series of prisms, one inside the next. Each word, each phrase, each formal composition, and finally the text as a whole reflects the multiple uses of the Name, building divine speech act on top of divine speech act. From the smallest and simplest utterance to the most multifaceted, the text imitates and reproduces the central speech act of speaking like the deity, from the sound of an individual phoneme to the composite of all sounds of the entire text.

The concept of ascent that emerges from this analysis is not best described on causal lines; that is, simply in terms of cause and effect. Ascent is not something distinct from the hymns, not a place beyond them that follows upon their recitation. The ambiguity of the frames, reinforced by the arrangement of the subtexts, deliberately confuses the temporal schema of saying → seeing. For example, in section 5, Akiba states that he prayed, saw, and gave praise. The formula appended to this frame could be either the prayer said in order to ascend or the praise said after the ascent. The same words thus are both "cause" and "effect." Similarly, in the next section, Akiba reports his question, "Who can meditate on the heavens and say 'I saw?'" The enumeration that follows is both a meditation on the heavens and an affirmative answer to his question; that is, a "saying I saw." The point of this ambiguity is that the recitation does not only cause the ascent, it is the ascent. The praise that "does" an ascent is the same praise said during the ascent and said to verify the ascent.

Perhaps the most interesting passages in the text are those that reject the entire didactic process. In section 9, Akiba chides Ishmael for asking his question. Akiba states that, if Ishmael were pure, he would know the answer to his question, for being pure is equivalent to being in the seventh heaven, having learned the divine language. This is the most extreme "spiritualization" possible, whereby inner purity fills the place of instruction and action. Yet, the authors know no spiritual/cultic dichotomy. For them, the question is the encoding of divine and human status in modes of language use. They have built an entire world of words, in which the essence of each participant is what he does by talking. Speaking, thus, is the most "real" action. It indexes not the outward aspects of the person but the evidence of his inner self and his divine status.

CHAPTER FIVE

The Pragmatics of Ascent and the Problem of Ritual Language

Creating the Words for Ascent

Maaseh Merkabah's provocative exploration of special "words" and didactic models of ascent permits us to review the ritual language system that underlies the text and its formal enactment in the structures of the text and apply these findings to current debates about ritual language.

Hebrew Scriptures present the dramatic model of the creation through speech of Genesis, but how can the human practitioner capture that power? Human uses of transformational language are not widespread in the Scriptural texts.[1] There are the important exceptions of curses and blessings, and the latter form an important element in the ritual language system. But how can the efficacy of blessings be extracted, as it were, and directed toward other transformations?

With the introduction of the idea that the deity uttered his own name in creating the world, the divine power becomes available to the human speaker to the extent that the name is available. That is, by centralizing the transformational ability of divine speech in the particular linguistic unit "name," it is possible for humans to take that power and make use of it.

deity speaks name in creating

semantization	repragmatization
word = deed	word = name = deed
deity's words are deeds	all powerful words are names

The very notion of the Shem Ha-Meforash (the Exegeted Name) is closely connected to the emerging Name ideology.[2] Scholars have tried to discern which of the many names of the deity is referred to by the term and exactly how the root *PŘS* is best understood and translated. However, as a name for the Name, the term cannot be explained by pinpointing a unique name to which it refers or by finding the best translation. The terms crystalizes in a single unit the ideologies discussed so far. The term is a name for the Name, signaling that the Name is now itself an object of speculation and investigation. The Name can be referred to without being spoken. The term is a shorthand reference to the Name as a secret, forbidden, all-powerful instrument of creativity.

This conception of the Name has implications for exegesis as well as ritual. The necessity of explication or uncovering the hidden power of the Name creates a parallel between it and the larger text. The named-Name is now the icon (image, pattern) by which all verbal compositions are measured and judged. They derive value to the extent that they are copies of that pattern. The Torah is described as a collection of names, enhancing the "magical" status of the text.[3] This is a mutually reinforcing relationship; the more powerful the Name, the more powerful the text, and vice versa. Exegesis of either "text" becomes a process not only of investigating semantic meaning but also of capturing the power of the words.

The solution to this problem is found in the shift from an ideology of divine language as spoken (Thus says the Lord), to an ideology of the power of the written text (the text containing the tokens of "Thus says the Lord" is itself a powerful object). The text is objectified as a collection of powerful words and at the same time the transformational power is located in the very name of the deity. Long after the deity spoke, the words are still available on earth, but now in the form of their written encapsulation in the text. The text is a receptacle of that divine speech. The words by which the world was created, along with many other examples of divine speech, are contained in the text. Each "Thus says the

Lord" is an utterance of divine speech and the text is a collection of these utterances.

The Aramaic Targums articulate a step in this process, perhaps in part because the process of translation objectifies the text. The addition of the Aramaic word for *Word*, for example, draws attention both to the fact that God's power was represented on earth by his effective speech and that the words he spoke are contained in that very text.[4] The Torah is a collection of tokens of divine speech, embodying the deity on earth, and as embodying implies, representing in physical (written) form the divine speech (spoken). The translations make the text itself a fetish, highlighting the latent power of the text.

Prohibitions against speaking the Name are not meant to place the ritual speaker in a quandary. Instead, restrictions that surround the Name are to be expected, for they are the result of the very power the Name contains. It is due to the privotal role of the name that such restrictions are necessary. If indeed automatic utterance of the Name encapsulates the creation process, it is not to be freely or regularly used. On the contrary, the more important the Name becomes, the more highly confined and restricted it will be. Therefore, the prohibitions surrounding its usage, reveal the central problem and also the key: how to develop and at the same time protect the ritual language system.

Creating the Forms for Ascent

The process of achieving and teaching ascent begins with a dilemma. The word that is the nucleus of the system is surrounded by taboos. The utterance of the Name is forbidden to those who wish to use it. This would seem to be an unsolvable dilemma. The pragmatics of divine speech are beyond their grasp, for the most effective word is also the only word that cannot be said. The process of speaking the Name is always fraught with the possibility of blasphemy. How then can they make use of the Name when it is not permitted to be uttered?

Constraints imposed by this complex and seemingly contradictory name ideology may correlate with the employment of certain forms within the text. For example, layered frames of reported speech mitigate charges of blasphemy by distancing the rabbis from the direct speaking of the formulas. How can it be wrong to merely repeat what the heavenly chorus has said? Even more important, however, is the development of a whole lexicon of Name-substitutes. The great variety of "Names" derives from the most divine Name, yet none of them are that most secret, most mysterious Name. God's Name can be used in the form of all the Namelike work that together establish a collection equivalent to the Name. The most powerful Name is beyond use, but endless formal and functional "partials" can be spoken as substitutes.

The ascent is effected in the forms and arrangements of the text, as well as the "message" conveyed in the semantic content. Unlike a handbook, the text does not merely direct an individual to carry out certain actions. Instead, it gives examples of the actions and speaks as though the actions were unfolding. The investigations into language are carried out both explicitly and implicitly. In certain sections, the role of language is discussed and described openly, for example when Nehunya says, "Everyone who prays this prayer in all his power can catch sight of the splendor of the presence" (lines 996-997). Here Nehunya describes a mode of language usage and correlates it with a specific result. Yet, at the same time that the text talks about the efficacy of language, it also presents implicit models of that efficacy at its most highly charged; the most potent of such language uses are instantiated, enabling the text to instruct by example.

Activities discussed in the text are interchangeably talked about and accomplished. To say the word *praised* is to praise; to say the word *blessed* is to bless. At this level, the issue is less controversial, for, as Silverstein explains, transformations encoded in a single word, especially a verb, are more transparent to the user and to the scholar of ritual language as well.[5] Similarly, to say the word *song* as part of a highly repetitive and rhythmic composition is to perform song. The simultaneity of speech and action, once established at the level of word = deed, operates at the level of the rite itself. To talk about ascent is to ascend, for the procedure cannot be conveyed without also conveying the experience.

The dilemma of Scholem and Gruenwald stems in part from the standard practice of relegating efficacious speech to the magic end of the religion-magic spectrum. Pragmatic analysis of *Masseh Merkabah* shows that distinctions between magic and religion cannot be sustained on the grounds of linguistic usage. The introduction of pragmatics shifts the basis of discussion away from, for example, compulsive versus petitionary dicotomies, which imply misused, or ill-applied language, to the study of the relation between linguistic forms and native ideologies. Once the issue is argued with functional approaches, linguistic usages will not fall neatly into the category either of magic or religion. The linguistic strategies are neither religious nor magical but instead appropriate to the specific problems that need to be solved in order to ascend and to communicate ascent. The native understanding of language presumes a difference between human and divine speakers, not magical and nonmagical forms. A pragmatic analysis assumes the transformative ability of language; a magic versus religion distinction therefore is not useful regarding the particular perceptions of this text.

This is not to deny that rabbinic texts reflect notions of proper and improper uses of powerful languages and actions. They make distinctions between actions that are simply illusions and those that reflect actual results based on invoking the wrong power or the wrong person doing the invoking. Even the names of other deities have power. But that does not mean, simply put, that the rabbinic notion should be the scholarly one. That is, just because the rabbis make distinctions in the control and use of supernatural powers, this does not mean that religion and magic do in fact exist as the neatly oppositional entities the rabbis describe.

The Name could be used for a variety of ends, but if the Name is the creative word par excellence, then ascent is the ritual par excellence. Creation from the letters of the deity's name is the deity's action; by trying to ascend the individual hopes to achieve the ultimate blasphemy, to be transformed into another type of being. As heretical as this idea is, it is even directly stated on numerous occasions, presumably because it is so hard to achieve. For example, Psalms 69:18 is interpreted in light of Proverbs 16:15 as meaning that the result of a heavenly vision is the achievement of immortality.[6] This goal can be reached the long way, learning all of Torah, the Name writ large, or by learning the Name, the Torah writ small. The "second birth," ascribed by Rabbi Judah ben Ilai to the one who hears the Name, is compared to knowing the entire Torah and is a birth from which there is no death.[7] All of Israel had the chance to gain that immortality in the wilderness, when the Name was still manifest and accessible. But the Name that gives immortality was lost.

In the classification of ascent texts developed by Tabor (1986, 69ff), *Maaseh Merkabah* appears to qualify as the type ascent as a foretaste of the heavenly world. Grasping the lessons of ascent transforms the student into a "son of the world to come" (line 84).[8] Tabor has classified *Hekhalot Rabbati* similarly, following the lead of Gershom Scholem Tabor (1986; 89). To be a son of the world to come means, presumably, to gain that chance at immortality available to those who know the Name.

Current Study of Ritual Language

If pragmatic analysis can contribute alternate means of analyzing structural equivalence, it is worthwhile to review the conclusions from this study about repetition, especially in relation to the functionality of language. This was Hoffman's starting point, and indeed current study of ritual language revolves to a great extent around the question of repetition, both within an individual event and from event to event.

As we have seen, and as Hoffman so clearly argues, narrowly defined semantic analysis has not been able to account for the function or structures of ritual language. Dissatisfaction with semantic analysis has motivated the growing interest in "performativity." Speech-act theories have been used to develop a special subset of speech acts, whose primary function is not to communicate information but to situate the speaker in a particular social context. For Wheelock, "stressing the creative potential of ritual language – that is, its ability to invoke the context – prevents the category mistake of regarding utterances simply as conveyors of information" (1982, 50). The realization that speakers generally use language for purposes other than reference and predication opens up new possibilities for ritual language as well. "The majority viewpoint . . . seems to be that the competence to speak any language involves at least two distinct though interlacing systems: a 'syntactico-semantic' component and a 'pragmatic' component, the latter dealing with how to use language in a social context" (1982, 50).

Here Wheelock advances an issue that Hoffman does not discuss; that is, if linguistic units have more than one function, what is the relation among these dimensions or, as Wheelock calls them, systems? As we saw in the case of Hoffman's study, the pragmatic component is often called upon to explain usages that appear to be semantic nonsense. Thus, the interlacing of these subsystems is often considered corollary in that one dimension operates at the expense of the other. In this regard Hoffman, Wheelock, and other scholars, such as Maurice Bloch (1974), all highlight the pragmatic component to the denigration of the semantic component. That is, the language of ritual does not, and should not, mean anything because it is filling other functions.

Bloch's argument about traditional oratory is reminiscent of Hoffman's discussion of liturgy. Block believes that much traditional oratory has no propostional force at all; that is, the semantics of traditional speech, like rabbinic liturgy, could be nonsense. It is the pragmatic implications of the words, not their meaning, that is important. In Bloch's case, semantic meaning is not necessary because the primary goal of traditional oratory is to provide coercive force for political authority admitting no challenge to that authority.

Bloch's particular version of this debate is important because it is typical of this approach, and even more so because it has elicited the careful criticism of Tambiah, in his article "A Performative Approach to Ritual." We will examine Tambiah's investigation in some detail, for he provides the most complete and well-argued statement about the relation of semantics and pragmatics. His contributions then can be contrasted with the findings from this study.

Tambiah questions the manner in which the interlacing of the functions often are characterized and criticizes Bloch for drawing too sharp a distinction between the components. According to Tambiah, Searle, who was one of the first and foremost proponents of speech act theories, argued that "In speech acts the propositional locutionary aspect is usually present but is embedded within the illocutionary act, not that there is an inverse variation between them" (Tambiah 1979, 151).

That is, according to Searle, the propositional dimension of language is part of its pragmatic capacity; one function is not at the expense of another. Tambiah therefore rejects Bloch and other scholars who turn to pragmatics as a means of dismissing semantics.[9] However, Tambiah ultimately does not move far from that position in his own theoretical descriptions of the functions of ritual language. Pragmatics, we find, is still used as an explanation for phrases and usages that seem to be semantically meaningless. For example, according to Tambiah, participants in a ritual effect social goals at the expense of meaning what they say, again denying the semantic component and elevating pragmatic meaning to the only type of meaning. Semantics and pragmatics are oppositional; as a text becomes "traditional" and is reused over a long time period, it loses its semantic value. Participants tend to be less and less concerned with what the text says, until its meaning on that level is lost. The text, however, continues to have pragmatic functions.

During these periods of ossification, rituals may increasingly lose whatever semantic meaning they previously had and may carry primarily indexical meanings that derive from rules of use and from pragmatic or functional considerations (1979, 165).

For Tambiah, the study of rituals involves tracing the fluctuations between these functions of language, as a ritual shifts from primarily filling one function to another. Revivals in rituals are resurgences in the semantic level of meaning and represent the opposite pole from ossification.

> One of our tasks, then, is to specify the conditions under which rituals – which ordinarily convey both symbolic and indexical, referential and pragmatic meanings – take opposite turnings: to the right when they begin to lose their semantic components and come to serve mainly the pragmatic interests of authority, privilege, and sheer conservatism; and to the left when committed believers, faced with a surfeit of manipulated "implications" strive to infuse purified meaning into traditional forms, as often happens during the effervescence of religious revival and reform. (1979, 166)

However, in *Maaseh Merkabah*, linguistic units have pragmatic force to the extent that they are equated semantically with the Name. Thus the functions of language (semantic meaning and pragmatic implications) are not oppositional. Instead, they are virtually synonomous; the process of defining the supposed semantic content is also the process of delimiting the pragmatic potential.

Tambiah himself moves beyond the model of right toward semantics and left toward pragmatics. The main thrust of Tambiah's article turns to the Piercean sign system in order to articulate the multifunctionality of language. Ritual has a "duplex existence," representing, either iconically or symbolically, the cosmology and at the same time having what we would call pragmatic entailment and presuppositions, as it "indexically legitimates and realizes social hierarchies."

> the value of the concept of indexical symbol and indexical icon for us is that they will enable us to appreciate how important parts of a ritual enactment have a symbolic or iconic meaning associated with the cosmological plane or content, and at the same time how those same parts are existentially or indexically related to participants in the ritual, creating, affirming, or legitimating their social positions and powers. (1979, 154)

Here we find methods of analysis similar to those of Silverstein's theories of poetic text pragmatics. The "iconic meaning associated with the cosmological plane" is manifest in the repeated layers of the text that reflect the cosmic layers. These dimensions of the text are the easiest to spot and are frequently noted in discussions of ritual language, though the terminology "iconic" is not widely used. The important point here is that the diagrammatic icons of the heavens do not simply describe the heavens but invoke the context for the rite.

Tambiah's indexical signaling related to "creating, affirming, or legitimating . . . social positions and powers" is in part the signaling of the special status of the ascender. In *Maaseh Merkabah*, linguistic equivalents of ideological formations are especially clear because the ideological formations (distinctions between human beings and divine figures) are always perceived in linguistic terms (special modes of speech). Thus, a context is prepared for the manipulation of ideological formations and for the transfer of divine language to human beings that accomplishes the rite.

At first, the text seems to be complex and disorganized, with phrases and words arranged in a random manner. However, pragmatic analysis readily demonstrates that the text in fact is an elaborate diagram of the Name in its many manifestations. The forms are not random; indeed, all elements are generated out of and, thereby, determined by the Name. The text thus is the opposite of arbitrary, with each linguistic unit motivated by the Name. Units not connected with the Name are factored out as much as possible.

If we return to Tambiah's statement about the iconic meaning associated with the cosmological plane of content, we can point out that the iconic meanings of ritual texts are not limited to cosmological issues. That is, whereas in *Maaseh Merkabah*, it often is the cosmological constructs that most readily appear to be icons, the iconicity of ritual texts in fact is more complex and extensive. With the aid of Jakobson's studies on parallelism, we are able to find multiple patterns, which in the case of ritual texts, provide icons of the very transformation toward which the rite is directed. In other words, when a ritual text is seen as an instance of the poetic function of language, it becomes doubly meaningful as both an index of the desired transformation and an icon of it as well. *Maaseh Merkabah*, with its lush descriptions of the heavenly realm and manipulations of the divine Name, is similar to a performative verb such as *promise*, writ small in the efficacious sounds and writ large in the text as a whole. It can communicate to us about the transformation of ascent, while at the same time enacting it. Thus, Tambiah leads us in the right direction but limits himself too much as regards the iconicity of ritual texts.

Tambiah returns us to the problem of repetition by arguing that the repetitive dimension of ritual language is explained in part by the importance of the conceptions that the rite addresses. Since the basic worldview of the community is portrayed and enacted in the articulation of the cosmology, it cannot and should not be altered easily. "If cosmological constructs are to be taken on faith and be considered as immutable, then it is a necessary corollary that the rites associated with them be couched in more or less fixed forms, be transmitted relatively unchanged through time and be repeatedly enacted on ordained or crisis occasions" (1979, 121-123).

Tambiah cites the work of Moore and Myerhoff and their definition of ritual as a "traditionalizing instrument," lending the aura of eternal truth to what in fact are only social constructs.

> These last authors make the telling observation that even in the case of a newly invented ritual (or ritual performed only once) it is constructed in such a way that "its internal repetitions of form and content make it tradition-like" because "it is supposed to carry the same unreflective conviction as any traditional repetitive ritual ..." (pp. 8-9). (1979, 123)

Even as Tambiah presents these opinions, he seems to realize that the usefulness of these explanations is limited. The notion that a text must be repeated solely to reinforce its message or to make a social worldview more emphatic still implies misused language. We have not come as far from Bloch's "broken record" theory of ritual language as Tambiah's criticism should have led us.

Emphasis upon the creativity of ritual texts as diagrammatic icons demands a new characterization of repetition in general. Once the repetitions internal to a ritual text are seen as supplying information about the rite by their very arrangement, the role of repetition can be described more accurately. Repetition is not employed in order to make instant tradition. Instead, it is the rigidity at one level of language (arrangement of forms) that permits creativity at another (ritual transformation).

In *Maaseh Merkabah*, the precise and highly parallelistic poetic arrangements of the hymns admit one dimension of the creative capacity of the rite. *Creative* does not mean spontaneous, original, or novel. Instead, *creative* is used as a technical term, related to the ability of a rite to bring about the goals toward which the rite is directed.

Consciously or not, the framers of this text have found a means of teaching lessons that cannot be communicated easily. It is not possible to explain ascent, for religious experiences are difficult to communicate, like the pearls of many-columned Iram that, outside of the city, appear to be only pebbles. In order to understand, the student himself must ascend, enter the city. In this text, the forms of reported speech and their specific arrangements are utilized in such a way to make the speech didactic, but so perfectly didactic that the gap between student and pedagogue, between pedagogy and experience, closes automatically. In travelling through these words, so radiantly potent with the Name, in speaking them to himself, each student's experience becomes so much like that of the teacher that the student becomes the teacher, the most successful notion of teaching possible.

Rabbi Akiba, annoyed at Rabbi Ishmael's persistent questions about what he should say to ascend, retorts that if Ishmael was pure, he would not have to ask so many questions. Because that transformation had not yet occurred, he was left only with language, with questions. Since divine power is contained in divine language, language alone can suffice to accomplish inner transformation, This inner transformation achieved, all forms of language become redundant.

APPENDIX ONE

The Textual Evidence

Study of the Hekhalot texts, while still in the early stages, has benefited from the recent appearance of Schaefer's *Synopse zur Hekhalot-Literatur*. This new edition of the major Hekhalot texts contains descriptions of the manuscripts and, in the case of *Maaseh Merkabah*, a presentation of five manuscript versions. Utilizing the tools provided by Schaefer, we will survey the manuscript evidence, textual divisions (major variants, minor variants), coherence of the textual content, and problems in translation.

The Manuscript Evidence

While Scholem was the first to edit a version of *Maaseh Merkabah*, his edition is a composite of two manuscripts and thus represents neither an actual manuscript nor a critical edition. For this reason, the text chosen as the basis for this investigation is one of the five manuscripts assembled by Schaefer. He includes brief introductions to these manuscripts, supplying data about their present location, date, length, style of handwriting, contents, and organizations.[1]

New York Manuscript (NY 8128)

This manuscript is Jewish Theological Seminary 828 (8128 according to the Kabbalah collection on microfilm). Schaefer describes this manuscript as a 224 page manuscript from the circles of the German Hasidim. Scholem dates the text to the end of the fourteen century or the beginning of the fifteen century. However, Schaefer also mentions a private communication from Beit Arie which supports an early sixteen century date. While Schaefer thinks that the manuscript may reflect the work of more than one person, he states that a more exact analysis is not possible based on the microfilm copy from which he worked.

113

Oxford Manuscript (O 1531)

This manuscript is Bodleian Library, Michael 9 = Neubauer (Catalogue of the Hebrew Manuscripts in the Bodleian Library, Oxford 1886). The manuscript contains 185 pages and also comes from the circles of the German Hasidim. It is dated by both Scholem and Beit Arie to the fourteen century.

Muenchen Manuscript (M 22)

This manuscript, Bayerische Staatsbibliothek, Cod. Hebr. 22, contains 224 pages, is in part written in an "Italian cursive" style, and is dated by Steinschneider (Die Hebraeischen Handschriften, p. 8f.) to the middle of the sixteenth century.

Dropsie Manuscript (D 436)

This manuscript, Dropsie University, Philadelphia, no. 436, with thirty-nine folios, is written in a Sephardic hand and is dated by Beit Arie to the fifteenth century. Schaefer decided that the folios were arranged incorrectly and rearranged them into a more logical order in his edition of the text. For example, *Maaseh Merkabah* is found in folios 33a-35b, 38a-38b, 32b, 32a, 31b, 31a, 37a-37b, and 36a-36b.

Muenchen Manuscript (M 40)

This manuscript, Bayerische Staatsbibliothek, Cod. Hebr. 40, with 227 pages, was written by three different people. The date 1547-48 appears in the third part of the manuscript, while Beit Arie dates the part of the manuscript with the Hekhaloth material to the end of the fifteenth century. These sections are written in an Ashkenasic script.

Schaefer does not claim that any one of these versions represents the "original" version of *Maaseh Merkabah*. Instead, he argues that the redaction stage occured late in the process of transmission. This fluid or, as he states, corrupt history of transmission eliminates the possibility of creating a critical edition (1981, v). Schaefer compares the problems encountered with these texts to those found in the study of Midrashic texts.

> A critical edition in the classic sense must not only arbitrarily choose one manuscript as the base text, it will also demand a series of excessively inflated variant apparati and will record in often alternating manuscripts readings "better" than the base text. The reader would therefore be forced to wander constantly between the base text and type apparatus, and to check all the variants because each manuscript in concrete cases offers a "better" reading. (1981, v-vi)[2]

Based in part on Schaefer's warnings about a critical edition, the present investigation is carried out on a single manuscript, N 8128. Schaefer uses this manuscript as the base text for his *Synopse* because it is the longest version and includes most of the material from the other manuscripts. He does not select the text because it clearly is the best, stating quite plainly that length is its main recommendation (1981, vi). He does note, however, in his article on *Merkabah Rabba*, that the New York and Oxford manuscripts contain specific examples of better readings (1977, 65). He concludes that, in text editions, these manuscripts should be used as the base texts, with the other versions included in the critical apparatus. Because the Oxford manuscript does not appear to be substantially superior to the New York one, this translation is based almost entirely on the New York version, with the variants included in the notes.

The selection of one manuscript to form the basis of the investigation is important for the claims of the study. If we follows Schaefer's lead and abandon the search for a critical edition, how then do we approach the text? For the purpose of this study N 8128 is analyzed as one example of *Maaseh Merkabah*. We do not wish to make the text less complex than it is, or simplify the textual history, or worse yet conduct the study on a scholarly construct that exists only within the bounds of the study. Therefore, we will view the New York manuscript as one version, perhaps even an interpretation by the copyist, of the more diverse group of texts collectively called *Maaseh Merkabah*.

Before turning to the variants, it should be mentioned that the New York manuscript contains non-Hekhalot materials in addition to *Hekhalot Rabbati* (The Greater Hekhalot), *Hekhalot Zutrei* (The Lesser Hekhalot), *Ḥarbe d'Moshe* (Sword of Moses), and assorted other Hekhalot paragraphs (1981, x-xiv). All this Hekhalot material is found on folios 1-43b. The next few folios (44a-51b) are ripped out, according to Schaefer, and the rest of the manuscript (51a ff.) is devoted to later kabbalistic texts. In comparison, the Oxford manuscript is much more complex in its general organization, with sections from texts interspersed with each other and with seemingly fragmentary material (1981, ix).

Textual Division and Variants

Scholem divided his 1967 edition of the text into thirty-three sections. Although he did not specify the criteria used in distinguishing these sections, they are not controversial. The text falls into fairly distinct units. Almost all thirty-three sections begin with the same patterns "Rabbi X said." The only exceptions are sections 27-31, which are the five formulas "arranged" for Ishmael by Nehunya. Each of these is introduced in the New York manuscript by the pattern, "The first, second, etc. prayer"; the divisions are marked less clearly in the other manuscripts. Schaefer's divisions of the paragraphs coincides almost exactly with Scholem's, though in several instances he subdivides Scholem's units into smaller parts.[3] In four cases (sections 14, 16, 24, and 31), we have also chosen to subdivide the sections for the purpose of analysis, usually because Scholem includes the pat-

terns "Rabbi X said" more than once in a section.[4] We have retained Scholem's
numberings and label the subdivisions 26A, 26B, etc.

In order to facilitate analysis, the text is further subdivided into 1153 lines.
In the case of the nonhymnic (framing) lines, the specific line length is to some
extent arbitrary. The introductory "Rabbi X said," is highlighted by having its
own line, and the switching of speakers often begins a new line. In the case of
the hymnic material, the text is divided to best present the parallel and poetic
constructions; that is, to highlight the Hebrew "feet."

Major Variants

M 22

M 22 differs from the other manuscripts in three places: (1) it skips from the
end of section 17 to the beginning of section 32; (2) it has a longer formula in
section 4; and (3) it adds two additional paragraphs after section 5. Variant 1 is
probably the most important, because a major portion of the text is missing. The
variant follows the sectioning of the text exactly, that is, the last word before the
gap is the last word of section 17 and the first word after the gap is the first word
of section 31. At first glance, the variant might appear to be due to scribal error,
for the same phrase occurs at the end of section 17 and at the end of section 31
(catch sight of the presence). The copyist might have simply skipped from the
first to the second occurrence of that phrase and lost the intervening sections.
However, it is important to note that the second occurrence of the phrase is found
only in the New York manuscript. The entire section (31) is missing in two manuscripts, M 22 and D 436. In the case of O 1531, the second half of the section,
the part containing the phrase, is represented only by the brief phrase "it is
beloved to him". If four of the manuscripts lack the second occurrence, can we
claim scribal error as the most likely explanation? It appears that the end of section
17 marks a major seam in the text, for here N 8128 adds the Aramaic sections
(18-20) and even without these additions, section 17 does not easily lead into
section 21. If the intervening sections missing from M 22 (21-31) are a later addition, then some of the Nehunyan sections (7, 11-17) were added to the Akiban
materials before others (21-31).

Finally, the phasing of section 17 would lead one to expect a single prayer
("pray a prayer," line 614) to appear between sections 17 and 31. However, this
"original" reading, with a single prayer, is found in none of the manuscripts,
including the shortest version, M 22. The last word of section 17 in M 22 is
followed by ". . .", signifying that the line is incomplete.[5] It seems likely, therefore, M 22 is an excerpt from a longer version, though that version may not be
exactly like any of the other manuscripts.

The other variants in M 22 are both additions of textual material. This manuscript has a general tendency to expand the text, as witnessed by the numerous
small additions of words and phrases (see variants). These variants are slightly
more extreme versions of ideosyncratic marking of M 22, which continually

lengthens the text. These additions tend to repeat standard phrases rather than introduce new types of textual material.

D 436

This manuscript is missing several of the lines of the formula in section 16 and, more important, it skips from the middle of the formula in section 30 to the end of section 32. THe break in section 30 coincides with the bottom of the page. Given the extensive disorder in the arrangement of the pages (see p. 114), it is more probable that the gap resulted from the loss of part of the manuscript.

N 8128

The New York Manuscript has three sections (18-20) that are not found in any of the other manuscript. These sections are written entirely in Aramaic. Although there are a few Aramaic phrases in other sections, the use of Aramaic for complete sections immediately sets them apart from the rest of the text. Also, the introductory frames mimic those of the rest of the text but are not successful in integrating the material. For example, section 20 begins "Ishmael said to Akiba." This pattern, while reminiscent of the reported-speech frames from the rest of the text ("Rabbi X said"), is not found elsewhere in the text.[6] Finally, the goals toward which the formulas in these sections aspire are only indirectly related to ascent. They are concerned in part with not forgetting learned material, and their thematic similarity to sections 11-16 may explain their placement after those sections. In light of their apparent status as an addition and their absence from all the other versions, these sections will not be included in the analysis.

Sources and Parallels

In addition to the citation of standard biblical passages about heavenly vision[7] *Maaseh Merkabah* shares entire passages with other Hekhalot texts. Two examples of these parallels, from *III Enoch* and *Merkabah Rabba*, reveal the manner in which each Heklahot text adapts material for its own purpose.

Gruenwald (1980, 181, n.2) and Alexander (1983, 304, n.a) both draw attention to the parallel to *Maaseh Merkabah* (3, 4, and 10) found in *III Enoch* 22B-C. In his edition of *III Enoch*, 22B-C is in an appendix because of their obvious status as additions. As is often the case with Hekhalot texts, we cannot claim direct borrowing in either direction, for we do not know when these sections were added to *III Enoch* or if they were found in a third text.

The parallel in *III Enoch* is as follows:

> 22B. (1) R. Ishmael said: Metatron, Prince of the Divine Presence, said to me: How do the angels stand on high? He said to me: Just as a bridge is laid across a river and everyone crosses over it, so a bridge is

laid from the beginning of the entrance to its end, (2) and the ministering angels go over it and recite the song before YHWH the God of
Israel. In his presence fearsome warriors and dread captains stand. A
thousand thousand and myriad chant praise and laud before YWHW,
God of Israel.

(3) How many bridges are there? How many rivers of fire? How
many rivers of hail? How many treasuries of snow? How many wheels
of fire? (4) How many ministering angels? There are twelve thousand
myriads of bridges, six above and six below; twelve thousand myriads of
rivers of fire, six above and six below; twelve thousand treasuries of
snow, six above and six below; twenty-four thousand myriads of wheels
of fire, twelve above and twelve below, surrounding the bridges, the rivers of fire, the rivers of hail, the treasuries of snow and the ministering
angels. How many ministering angels are at each entrance? Six for every
human being, and they stand in the midst of the entrances, facing the
paths of heaven. (5) What does YHWH, the God of Israel, the glorious
king, do. The great God, mighty in power, covers his face. (6) In Arabot
there are 660 thousands of myriads of glorious angels, hewn out of flaming fire, standing opposite the throne of glory. The glorious King covers
his face, otherwise the heaven of Arabot would burst open in the middle,
because of the glorious brilliance, beautiful brightness, lovely splendor,
and radiant praises of the appearance of the Holy One, blessed be he.
(7) How many ministers do his will? How many angels? How many
princes in the Arabot of his delight, feared among the potentates of the
Most High, favored and glorified in song and beloved, fleeing from the
splendor of the Shekinah, with eyes grown dim from the light of the
radiant beauty of their King, with faces black and strength grown feeble?
Rivers of joy, rivers of rejoicing, rivers of gladness, rivers of exultation,
rivers of love, rivers of friendship pour out from the throne of glory,
and, gathering strength, flow through the gates of the paths of heaven
of Arabot, at the melodious sound of his creatures' harps, at the exultant
sound of the drums of his wheels, at the sound of the cymbal music of
his cherubim. The sound swells and bursts out in a mighty rush – Holy,
holy, holy, Lord of host, the whole earth is full of his glory.

22C. (1) R. Ishmael said: Metatron, Prince of the Divine Presence,
said to me: What is the distance between one bridge and another?
Twelve myriads of parasangs: in their ascent twelve myriads of parasangs, and in their descent twelve myriads of parasangs. (2) Between the
rivers of fear and the rivers of dread, twenty-two myriads of parasangs;
between the rivers of hail and the rivers of darkness, thirty-six myriads
of parasangs, between the chambers of hail and the clouds of mercy,
fourty-two myriads of parasangs, between the clouds of mercy and the
chariot, eighty-four myriads of parasangs; between the cherubim and the
ophanim, twenty-four myriads of parasangs; between the ophanim and
the chambers of chambers, twenty-four myriads of parasangs; between

the chambers of chambers and the holy creatures of the throne of glory, thirty thousand parasangs; (3) from the foot of the throne of glory to the place where he sits, forty thousand parasangs, and his name is sanctified there.

(4) The arches of the bow rest upon Arabot, a thousand thousand and a myriad of myriads of measures high, by the measure of the watchers and the holy ones, as it is written, "I have set my bow in the clouds.". .

The parallel in 22B is almost exactly the same as section 3 of *Maaseh Merkabah*. However, in the next few lines (22:5-6) the question from section 4 is supplied in *III Enoch* with a different answer. The question What does the deity do? elicits the answer that he covers his face. In *Maaseh Merkabah*, the question is repeated and rephrased, connecting it with the prior description of the angels (How is it possible to catch sight of them and . . . the deity does). The answer is complex, containing instructions on the use of the great mystery and an appended hymn. The answer, like the reformulated question, addresses two topics, how to catch sight of the heavenly creatures, and what the deity does (deals righteously and stands on his behalf).

The answer in *III Enoch* resembles more closely the answer to the previous question, which lacks an appended hymn and instructions. In this sense it may be "original." The answer in *Maaseh Merkabah* reflects the "redaction" of the section for the ascent text. Here we catch a glimpse of the special emphasis of *Maaseh Merkabah*, which moves away from the descriptive – how the deity covers his face – to the ritual question – the actions of the ascender and the deity.

However, this is not to argue that *III Enoch* shows no signs of redaction. Alexander states that the opening originally included a question from Ishmael (How do the angels stand on high?) followed by the answer of the heavenly mentor (He said to me). As it stands, the reference to Metatron has been added to the frame in order to make the opening resemble the other frames more closely.

The parallel in 22C is again almost identical to *Maaseh Merkabah*, outlining the heavenly bridges and the layout of the heavenly realm. *III Enoch* then shifts to an exegetical section, interpreting the biblical passage "I have set my bow." This exegetical passage may have been placed after the early verses of 22C because it continued the theme of measurement. In both texts, however, there is a distinct transition after the phrase "his name is declared holy there." The arrangement of *III Enoch* shows that at least one redactor ordered the passages as section 3, section 4 with a different answer, and then section 10. The idea that these three sections are related is shown by the similarity in the phrasing of the question (How . . .) without needing the testimony of *III Enoch*. It reinforces the likelihood that all Akiban sections do not represent a single source. Additionally, *III Enoch* 23 and 24 with their "how many" questions are closer examples of sections like *Maaseh Merkabah* 3, 4, and 10, which might provide help in interpreting those sections.[8]

Another Hekhalot text, *Merkabah Rabba*, contains parallels from two sections in *Maaseh Merkabah*; paragraphs 675-76 include lines from the first section of *Maaseh Merkabah* and paragraphs 677-78, lines from *Maaseh Merkabah* section 11.

675. Rabbi Ishmael said: Happy is the man who will complete this secret from morning to morning, acquiring the world and the world to come. Blessed is he on the throne, high and exalted. You dwell in the chambers of the heights, the palace of loftiness because you revealed the secrets and the secrets of the secrets and the mysteries and the mysteries of the mysteries.

676. You revealed to Moses and Moses to Joshua and Joshua to the elders and the elders to the prophets and the prophets to the righteous ones and the righteous ones to the heaven-fearers and the heaven-fearers to the people of the great assembly and from the people of the great assembly they were revealed to all of Israel and Israel used them to do by them Torah and make great learning (Talmud) and recite before them every secret. . . . Blessed are you Adonai, wise of all secrets and Lord of all mysteries.

677. Rabbi Ishmael said: I was thirteen years old, Rabbi Nehunya ben Hakana my teacher, saw that I was in a great affliction and in a great suffering and in great danger. I read the Mikra one day and I forgot it the next day. What I did as soon as I saw that Torah did not remain in my heart, I took myself and refrained myself and my soul from food and drink and bathing and anointing and I detained myself from the use of a bed and I did not talk and I did not converse neither a word nor a tune nor a song went forth from my lips.

678. Immediately Rabbi ben Hakana insisted to me ? and took me from the house of my father and led me to the cell of Gazith part of the temple and made me swear in the name of ZBWDY>L Adonai God of Israel and this is Metatron Adonai God of heaven and earth, God of the sea and God of the dry land. And he revealed to me immediately the secret of the Torah, enlightened my heart and the gates of the east and enlightened the wheels of my eyes in the dark places and the paths of Torah and nothing was forgotten from my mouth, everything my ears heard from the mouth of my rabbi and from the mouths of the students and in the paths of Torah which I did in them in their truth, again I did not forget.

Paragraphs 675-76 have a simpler speaking frame (no mention of Akiba) and connect recitation of the hymn with acquiring the world to come and not explicitly with ascent. The hymn also is longer; the long chain of teachers is reduced to Moses and the people of Israel in *Maaseh Merkabah*. The connection between this paragraph and the next may be the reference to Torah, which is the focus of Ishmael's problems in 677-678. By its placement before these paragraphs, and its distinct frame, the purpose of the prayer in this context is to increase learning.

Ishmael, in 677-678, is very distressed because he cannot remember his learning. He begins a strict regimen including neither eating nor sleeping. At this point Nehunya appears and takes him to the Temple and teaches him to make use of the "great oath." This solves Ishmael's problems and he immediately begins to remember everything he learns. In *Maaseh Merkabah* (section 11) some of the clarity of the setting is lost, and the reason for Ishmael's distress is not articulated. The conversation is hard to construe, as if the frame for the appended formula was incomplete or corrupt. As it stands, Nehunya reveals the prince of the countenance and then someone ("he") speaks to Ishmael. It is hard to tell if the speaker is still Nehunya, or if the information about the prince of the Torah is conveyed by the angelic figure mentioned (?) by Nehunya. The "redaction" of this frame for the context of *Maaseh Merkabah* is at least partly unsuccessful. The confusion may stem from adapting a frame with Nehunya as the teacher to be, instead, an angelic revelation.

In the case of the parallels to *Merkabah Rabba* 675-676, again we see the emphasis on ascent peculiar to *Maaseh Merkabah*; the hymn is directly connected with ascending. The material is arranged in a different order, but again, as in the case of *III Enoch*, it is not clear that *Merkabah Rabba*'s order is original either. *Merkabah Rabba* 677-678 has been changed from an extensive narrative to an incomplete bit of narrative introducing instructions and special formulas. The purpose of the appended formulas not only has been shifted to ascent, but it has been generalized. Instead of functioning for a one-time – and only one-time – problem of Ishmael, the special words are for everyone "who seeks him." Again, narrative has given way to ritual instruction.

The third important parallel, in this case not to another Hekhalot text, is the appearance in section 5 of the "Alenu." This prayer became part of the standard liturgy, though in a version that differs from the one found in *Maaseh Merkabah*. Thyehymn has fewer word and phrase parallels, less piling up of images, than most formulas in *Maaseh Merkabah*. Its extensive discussion of the earthly acceptance of God's rule also is unusual for the text. However, the hymn is linked closely with its present context by the word *praise*, which occurs in both the first line of the formula (153) and in the introduction (151). Perhaps, it is included in *Maaseh Merkabah* because it, too, constitutes a type of praise and therefore can be used in a manner similar to the other praise formulas. Several of the first person plural endings have been changed to the singular, as in the very first word (It is upon us → it is upon me). All of the plural endings, however, have not been changed, and the result is the awkward alternation between persons. The shift to the first person singular is consistent with the present context of the prayer, for here Akiba recites it individually. The lines of this prayer not found in the standard version (lines 165-67) are the lines most similar to the other hymns, due to their parallel placement of short, slightly altered praise phrases with divine names. These lines appear to modify the hymn for its present context and purpose.

All three examples demonstrate that, although the material is shared among more than one text, the parallels do not have the exact same wordings. The questions from *III Enoch*, in the context of *Maaseh Merkabah*, became questions about ascent. The temple location of the lesson from Nehunya in *Merkabah Rabba* is abandoned, and no location is mentioned. And even the Alenu, with the addition of the naming lines, is transformed for the context of *Maaseh Merkabah* and becomes an ascent hymn. These findings reinforce Schaefer's statements about the lack of an original and the problems with defining a better reading. Each of these readings is better for *Maaseh Merkabah*, but not better in relation to their occurrence in other texts.

Coherence of the Textual Content

The Nehunya-Ishmael didactic model differs from the Akiba-Ishmael model. We must presume that Ishmael learns from Akiba, although we never see him putting his lessons to use. When, however, Ishmael tells us that he learned something from Nehunya and then gives us further details by enacting the lessons exactly, we learn from Ishmael's lesson in a different way.

Section 17 appears to be a transition section, as Gruenwald interprets it (1980, 186). We find in this section references both to the "twelve words," which comes from the angel-summoning rite in section 11, and to a request for a vision of the deity. Both procedures are combined, or connected, leading the way from the descent of angels to the imparting of ascent information. This interpretation assumes that the phrase *twelve words* refers only to angel summoning.

It is possible that some of the other letter manipulations were at one point Aramaic phrases that become corrupt in the process of transmission. Note that the words have become letter clusters in M 40 (lines 403-404). These formulas are harder to analyze than most of the compositions in *Maaseh Merkabah* because their boundaries generally are less distinct; Hebrew instructions are mixed in with words to be spoken.[9] The Aramaic words are not the only difficulty in these sections, which stand out from the rest of the text as generally more complex to understand.

Nehunya's answer (section 17) to Ishmael, that he should pray a prayer, lacks an appended prayer. Section 31B also reads as if it were the closing for the issues raised in 17. Perhaps at some stage there was only one prayer between 17 and 31, and later it was expanded to the group of five. In this regard, it is interesting to note that the specific wording, "five prayers," appears in the New York manuscript only.

Placed directly in the middle of the angel-naming units are sections 24-25, which discuss the general eligibility for using the mystery. These two sections function in a manner similar to the discussion in section 1, where Akiba states that a "man" can recite the proper formula. Here, too, the criteria are simple – any person can recite the prayer.

What then is the relation between these procedures? Gruenwald notes that the illumination Ishmael received due to the descent of angels is very similar to that received during an ascent, or descent (1980, 187). They are both initiated by information (formulas, names) received from Nehunya. The specific reference to Ishmael's inability to remember what he learned is absent from section 11, so the purpose of the angel-summoning rite is not as clear as in the parallel *Maaseh Merkabah*. Instead of using the formula from section 11 to become an instant source of all Torah, as seen in the case of some formulas about forgetting, in this instance the purpose is much closer to the general illumination sought by the ascent hymns.

This breakdown of the text differs in part from Gruenwald's analysis. He chooses his divisions mainly on the basis of theme and distinguishes the Prince-of-the-Torah units, which he considers (11-22) distinct from the earlier and later hymnic sections (1-10, 23-31). As to his split at section 22, there is no reason for separating sections 21 and 22 from 23, for the theme of Ishmael's shining face expressly links 23 with 22. Our classification is based primarily on the distinction between those units where Akiba is the instructor and those where Nehunya fills that role. Thus section 7, because it includes Nehunya, is considered with the other Nehunyan sections, and the last two Akiban sections (32-33) are part of the general Akiban group, in spite of their appearance at the end of the text.

This theory, however, leaves unexplained the appearance of Akiba in section 25. In that section, an angel challenges Ishmael for elevating himself over his companions by saying that only he is privileged to make use of the secret revealed. In an appended comment, Ishmael claims that only he and Akiba are permitted to make use of the secret. However, the angel, in his attack, does not mention Akiba directly and phrases the question as if he were challenging only Ishmael, "Do not say 'Only I' am privileged above all." Perhaps the reference to Akiba was added to tie together the text, for once the dialogues are combined, it is clear that not only Ishmael is privileged in the secret. If, on the one hand, the appearance of Akiba would seem evidence of coherence with the Akiban and later sections, on the other hand, the same angel name is found in section 11. The similarity of this angelic discussion with the other weighs more heavily than the occurrence of Akiba in the section and we have therefore included this section with the Nehunya/angel units.[10]

If indeed the reference to Akiba was added, this is a rare sign of redaction. That is, the Nehunya-Ishmael and Akiba-Ishmael conversations are not fused in general. Instead the Nehunyan material is simply positioned among, almost framed by, the Akiban sections at the beginning (1-10) and at the end (32-33). Because the Akiban units jump from topic to topic within the broad theme of ascent – what does a man say? what did Akiba see? – the reader can easily move to the new rites and issues broached by Nehunya.

There are two separate problems within the topic of redaction: first, the inner changes made to the sections to incorporate them in their present setting in the text; and second, the sequencing of sections within the larger framework or structure of the text. As to the first question, it is possible to find evidence about the changes for the context of *Maaseh Merkabah* only in those instances where we have other versions of the material in other texts. These have been discussed already and include the special configurations of the parallels from *Merkabah Rabba*, *III Enoch*, and the Alenu as seen in this text. As to the second question, there are very few clues to why the sections are arranged in their pattern. The example of the close placement of the two citations of the heavenly chorus from Isaiah 6:3 (sections 6 and 7) may yield some evidence. That is, the Nehunyan section 7 may have been placed after the Akiban section 6 because both of them include the recitation of "holy, holy, holy." Ishmael, like Akiba, reports having seen the heavenly chorus, and he thereby can answer Akiba's question from section 6, "Who can say 'I saw?'" His "seeing," however, is now interposed within the larger ascent defined by the sections around it. In the previous section, the citation was said by the chorus in the first and then the second heaven. The recitation now becomes an ascent only to the second heaven.

If, in this case, content considerations may have dictated placement, there are few other examples of this phenomenon. Many of the units are self-contained.

They are comprehensible independent of the specific proceeding or subsequent section. This is true, for example, of many of the sections that raise a topic in the question and then answer it in the appended lines. Several of the procedures outlined by Nehunya supply a vague "plot," which develops from unit to unit.

Problems with Translation

The problems with translation vary between the Akiban and the Nehunyan sections. The former present very few difficulties, for the vocabulary is not extensive and is highly repetitions. The latter sections include more diverse vocabulary and several special problems, such as the letter manipulations and the Aramaic words.[11] Before turning to the specific problems of the Nehunyan sections, we will review two issues that affect the entire text: the inherent difficulties of translating verse and the problem of unclear imagery.

On the question of verse, the first issue is the division of poetic material into lines; that is, the problem of determining the Hebrew analogue of feet. Scholem, perhaps because of the difficulties inherent in this task, chose to print some sections as poetry and others as prose, even though the latter included formulas with poetic devices. In addition to the formulas highlighted by Scholem in sections 1, 4, 5, 9, 16, and 32, we include as formulas lines from 15, 27-31, and 33.[12] In the vast majority of all of these lines, the parallelistic construction dictates the line divisions. Scholem may have avoided printing these hymnic sections as poetry to separate them from the composition he considered prayers. Unlike the prayers, these compositions include at least a few lines of letter manipulations.

The line-lengths of all the formulas are not equally clear and, in some cases, this affects the translation. For example, in lines 1008-11 the addition or deletion of a word will result in a variant translation for several lines, for it alters the pattern of a series of phrases. The text is obscure as to which nouns belong together, and the wide variation again implies that each manuscript opts for a slightly different construction of a difficult clause. Problems in construing noun clauses are compounded by the nature of these hymns, for they string together many noun phrases, and in the process of transmission a single error can disrupt an entire parallelistic formation. In other cases, such as lines 104-45, where the parallelism is less distinct, lines are selected on the basis of phrasing, though the length of phrasing is not always equal: In them, ones of distinguishedness and powerfulness are complete, before you joy and happiness rise up. Where the image is less clear (is it a description of the chorus? the praising process?), it will be harder to divide the text into "feet," and textual corruption may be the cause.[13]

The strategy of translation employed here is to work from the examples of distinct parallelism, and then attempt to divide the remaining clauses as evenly as possible. This is not a widespread problem, and it is often possible to decide how to construe noun phrases by working from a clear image and taking the words before and after it as another noun phrases. Again, this is not to overstate the clarity of the text. In parts it is unreadable, and some lines are translated even though their import is vague (a watcher on land and shaker of it (?), line 1134).[14]

Finally, a constant problem in translating Hekhalot hymns is the selection of English equivalents for the extensive praise language. It is often hard to find English terms for the multiple Hebrew roots, and some of the choices, such as "songery" may seem forced. All occurrences of the same root are glossed with the same English translation, resulting in, for example, the root (HDR) majesty, forming the verbal *majestify*.

The problem of unclear imagery is seen, for example, in section 4. The last few lines present a picture of the number and arrangement of the angels in the heavenly realm, but this picture is corrupt. These lines do not seem to answer the question – how many angels? – except when they are emended by Alexander. He notes that the lines are unclear, and even with the emendation, the description of the angels is still hard to grasp (1983, 305, n. f.).

The same problems occur in the frames, and some of the speaking situations are preserved in such corrupt states that it is impossible to tell who is speaking to whom. The simple alteration of to me (LY) to to him (LW) can transform a frame and either make it meaningless or cause other lines to be emended as well. These particular problems are compounded by the use of abbreviations such as the common shortening of "Rabbi Ishmael said" to (')R'Y) and the use of (')'L) for "he said to him." These abbreviations are even easier to confuse and may contribute to some of the lack of clarity when impedes translation.

As to the special translation problems with the Nehunyan sections, the issue of Aramaic words has already been discussed. A complete study of the remaining issue, the letter clusters, is beyond the scope of this investigation. These sound clusters, a common device often characterized as "magical language," are simply transliterated and grouped into the word-length units seen in Schaefer's edition. Wherever it is possible to discern a Hebrew root, these are included in English after the letter cluster. The problem with translation is that these letter clusters are mixed with translatable phrases, and it is often hard to discern when it is best to translate a word and when it is best to include it as a transliteration. Where only one or two translatable words occur in the midst of letter clusters, they are presented as transliterations, for it is often impossible to develop them into any kind of phrase.[15]

Variations of Frames Within Maaseh Merkabah

The Nehunyan frames are in general more complex than the Akiban, in part because the formulas are interwined with instructions for their use. As a result, the frames repeatedly shift back to reported context from the reported formula, whereas in the Akiban sections the formulas are conclusions of the reported speech. This is especially true of those frames associated with the ritual for summoning angels. In the extreme cases of 11 and 13, it is not always possible to distinguish the prayers because they lack the boundary markers such as "This is the prayer" and "he prays." For example, in section 11, lines 403-408 are instructions that preface line 409, while lines 429-32 may be part of the formula or simply an appended comment. These frames are more likely to lack a formula entirely. In the Akiban sections, only section 2 lacks even the semblance of a formula; several Nehunyan sections have no formula at all. Where there is no formula, it is open to question whether they indeed are frames, for the narratives do not "frame" more deeply embedded material. However, they still have an outer narrative and reported content of a conversation.

The greater complexity of the Nehunyan frames raises the question of whether a different ideology is at work here; it is as if there were a need for more discussion in the presentation of the formulas. The frames present more detailed explanations of how the verbal compositions are to be used. It is important to note that, in the presentation of the formulas, a greater attempt is made to clarify how they are to be used. The formulas themselves are sometimes of a slightly different type, including letter manipulations and, on occasion, Aramaic.

The frames associated with the angel-summoning ritual and not ascent are closer to those of the Akiban section, again presenting the formulas as the most deeply embedded material and emphasizing the saying → seeing sequence. The borderline case appears to be in the recitation of angel names found in section 23, for on the one hand, it seems to be very close to the recitation that summons angels, while at the same time, the frame is similar to those that introduce ascent hymns. Here, the listing of names, like the listing of fiery chariots, indexes the individual's arrival at each gate.

As noted in Table 1, in several cases, the Nehunyan sections embody a variation of the dialogue theme, presenting not reported dialogues but summaries of dialogues. This switch is found in sections 7, 15, 22, 25, and 26C. Here the dialogues are removed from the reader, as it were, because the exact words are not reported. We are told, however, about the results the conversation or the results of the use of formulas learned during the conversation. Ishmael reports what happened to him when he put Nehunya's words to work. These summaries establish a more direct, or perhaps different, mode of conveying the efficacy of the words to the next speaker in the chain. They are correlated with a shift in the narrative, whereby Ishmael becomes the successful user of formulas he learned from others. The report of these usages demands a different type of frame.

Old Testament Theories of Language

Old Testament scholars have speculated at length about the role of words in Genesis and in other biblical passages, and it is worthwhile reviewing their debates in order to clarify both the problems and possibilities inherent in claims about native linguistic ideology. Procksch (1967), Grether (1934), Von Rad (1965), and other Old Testament theologians collected multiple illustrations of words with "special powers." They frequently cited, for example, "I am making my words in your mouth a fire" (Jeremiah 5:14) and "my word . . . shall not return to me empty" (Isaiah 55:11) as well as the creation story. Such unusual descriptions of words, according to these scholars, were part of the ancient Israelite worldview. Procksch argued that, unlike our culture, which has a dianoetic (thoughtbased) view of language, the Israelites had a dynamic understanding of language. Evidence for this dynamic view is found in the very word *davar*, which means both *thing* and *word*. Thus, for Procksch, "Every davar is filled with power which can be manifested in the most diverse ways" (1967, 92).

Similarly, Grether's famous study, *Name und Wort Gottes im Alten Testament*, includes a major section on the etymology of the word *davar*, attempting to show that an etymological investigation can help to explain the extraordinary function of the word in biblical texts (1934, 59-138).

Such explanations of biblical language have been severely criticized. To many scholars, these studies seemed to leave the ancient Israelites in a prelogical fog. Attacked by both theologians and linguists, these theories suffered a general demise along with much of the field of biblical semantics. For example, James Barr (1961) rejects the etymologically based explanations of the word *davar* by not only casting doubt on some of Gether's derivations but also pointing out that etymologies do not in fact determine usages of a word. Barr criticizes the sweeping contrasts between Greek and Hebrew thought that arose in the earlier studies, which were concerned largely with word/action speculations. "Like some others of these pieces of theological ethno-psychology, their use in relation to linguistic phenomena has it origin not in an observation Hebraic psychology, but in a misuse of fragments of Western and modern linguistic knowledge" (1961, 133).

Similarly, in his article, "The Supposed Power of Words in the Biblical Writings," A. C. Thiselton (1974) carefully dismantles these characterizations, offering four specific objections to biblical semantics. First, he reiterates Barr's generally accepted criticism of the ill-fated attempts at etymology. A large number of these reconstructions have turned out to be entirely speculative or simply wrong. Second, Thiselton argues that "powerful" words are usually spoken by a god or an individual with special authority, such as a king or a priest. "We suggest that a generalizing argument has misleadingly been put forward on the basis of select paradigms of a very special type" (1974, 283).

Here, he is correct and his objection is central. By pointing out that only the words of some speakers have these special effects, he highlights the extent to which scholars took the pattern of the deity's speech, for example, and applied it to all words. All utterances in the Bible do not function in the same fashion.

As a third point, Thiselton introduces Austin's notion of illocutionary acts, hoping that Austin's schema will offer an alternative to theories that present the Israelites as primitive or attempt to elevate this seeming confusion to a superior mode of thought.

> In performative utterances we have an example of the power of words in which word and event are indeed one, but not on the basis of some supposedly primitive confusion between names and objects. Neither ancient nor modern society depends on mistaken ideas about word magic in order to support the belief that words do things. (1974, 294)

Powerful words are always spoken by people of authority. The power is not so much in the words as in the person or institution behind these words, as noted in his second objection. In turn, for those persons for whom the model does fit, efficacy of their words is based on social convention not magic.

The fourth and last objection challenges the distinction between dynamic and dianoetic thought put forward by biblical theologians to demonstrate a difference between Hebrew and "Western" thought processes. This distinction, as with the etymologies, represented the more extravagant speculations of biblical theologians and, as Thiselton notes, depends on highly selective reading and interpretation of both Hebrew and Western texts.

Thiselton's objections are well taken, directed as they are at extreme interpretations of biblical semantics and at mystifying explanations of "rich usages." His arguments are worth reviewing because we can use them as guidelines to delimit our own claims about biblical view of language, there is no difference between words and deeds. It would be highly suspect to assert that there is any one view of language that uniquely warrants the label *the Biblical view*. However, this does not mean that the biblical texts contain no distinct models of special language use or that the native ideology can be explained on the basis of Austin. For example, when Thiselton questions Von Rad's statement that the Biblical view of language is actually richer than our own concept, he writes, the verdict forced upon us by modern general linguistics since the work of Saussure is that far from being "richer" such a view of words and things is certainly not "by nature" but rests on use, social traditions, rules of convention; on what Saussure himself called the first principle of language, namely, l'arbitraire du signe. (1974, 287)

This is a rather heavy-handed critique. Saussure's theory of the arbitrariness of the sign concerns the relation between words and objects and suggests that, at the level of linguistic theory, these native ideas simply are wrong. However, this does not negate influence of native concepts about language on the composition of texts and they often provide crucial insight into their intricacies. Such views are not simply "wrong," but instead provide a key to the function of words for the group that assumes them. That is, though linguistics may accurately advance the arbitrary relation between words and objects, this hardly exhausts the subject of the social roles of language. Native speakers are certain to have other ideas about language. The theoretical explanation of the arbitrariness of sense does not explain the force of reference as in speech acts.

This is not to say that the work of biblical scholars is correct. Von Rad, for instance, extrapolating from the example of Genesis, posits a too-general, all-pervasive relation between words and objects (or deeds) in the minds of the ancient Israelites. In criticizing Von Rad, Thiselton correctly has pointed to some vast overgeneralizations and overreachings in theological discussions about biblical language. But, in leading us correctly from sweeping statements about a single and unique biblical theory of language, Thiselton should be leading us toward a more variegated discussion of conventions of language within the text. This critique, however, should rest on a more careful reading of native ideas about words and deeds within the text and not on Saussure's comments about the arbitrariness of the sign.

If we then return to *Maaseh Merkabah*, what can be stated about the summations of divine speech such as "Creator of his world by his one name?" Within the limitations of this study, it is sufficient to argue that this represents a rabbinic interpretation of the creation story. We can lay aside much of the debate over biblical views, because we are dealing here with a rabbinic summation of the biblical story. This summation declares that the deity created the world through speech and that the specific speech he employed was his name. The second part of this idea, that he spoke his name, is clearly a rabbinic addition, for the creation story in Genesis does not state that God spoke his name. The first part must be dealt with carefully, for it seems that the text of Genesis can easily be read as supplying a word-deed model. After Thiselton's research, however, we must add that this is only one possible native ideology, and no doubt others operate in diverse passages. And this model itself belongs not to all speech but in the creation story only to speech of the deity. When the divine speaker states, "Let there be light," light exists, for in divine speech words translate into or entail deeds. Thiselton cites several examples of creation through speech by deities and mentions examples from other ancient Near Eastern texts. Whereas Thiselton would replace claims of biblical semantics with Austin's categories of excercitives, commissives, and other types of performatives, we would state instead that the Genesis text can be read as a model of divine speech, whereby the words of the deity become deeds. The deity in Genesis does not employ performatives but simply "says," which again may distinguish divine from other types of speech. This description of the model from Genesis does not lay claim to motivate all biblical ideas of divine and human words. The examples of prophetic words as well as the famous irrevocable blessings in Genesis 27 and Numbers 23 seem to represent other types of efficacious words.

This notion of a divine mode of speech that has direct efficacy does inform some biblical stories, such as Moses' striking of the rock in Numbers 20:2-13. God tells Moses to order the rock to give water; instead, he strikes it and is punished by not being allowed to enter the holy land. He ignored the specific command of the deity, who told him to take action by means of speech, for speech empowered by the deity can effect action. Moses, however, strikes the rock, negating or denying God's creative speech by instead using physical force.

Notes

Chapter One. Images of Ascent

1. See for example, Segal, 1980.

2. Among Scholem's writings, see in particular "Merkabah Mysticism and Jewish Gnosticism" (1941, 40-79) and *Jewish Gnosticism, Merkabah Mysticism and Talmudic Tradition* (1965).

3. This text was first published as an appendix to Scholem (1965a, 101-107). Scholem edited the text using two manuscripts, Oxford 1531 and New York 8128, dating the former to the fourteenth century and the latter, tentatively, to the early fifteenth century. Since his edition appeared, the text was republished in Schaefer 1981, this time presenting the New York and Oxford manuscripts in a synoptic version with three other manuscripts. Schaefer's edition will be the basis for this study. See his note on Scholem's edition (pp. vi-vii).

4. Gruenwald 1980, 99. This collection is the Hekhalot corpus that Scholem and Schaefer have delimited in different ways (see note 5). Since most of the texts have not been the focus of individual studies, it is too early to speculate whether they will represent similar practices and notions of ascent. This study will attempt to explain one particular text, without claiming that the text embodies the entire Hekhalot corpus.

5. Scholem's corpus included The Visions of Ezekiel, The Lesser Hekhalot, The Greater Hekhalot (Hekhalot Rabbati), Physiognomic Fragments, Maaseket Hekhalot, III Enoch, and Maaseh Merkabah. All of these are revelations about the heavenly realm, called *the chariot*, and all except the first are associated with Rabbis Akiba and Ishmael, as noted by Scholem (1965a, 7). For Schaefer's "corpus," see 1981, vi-vii.

6. For example, in editing his edition of *Maaseh Merkabah*, Scholem used one manuscript from the fourteenth century and added variants from another fourteenth, possibly fifteenth century, manuscript.

7. Among Christian texts, he mentioned Paul's ascent in II Corinthians and the Apocalypse of John. For Greek parallels, see 1965a, 23, n. 61.

8. On this point, see Schaefer's judicious comments (1981, v-vi). Scholem gave the title "Maaseh Merkabah" to his composite edition of two manuscripts of a very similar text. He chose this title because one line of the text is cited by Eleazar of Worms and attributed to a text called "Maaseh Merkabah" (line 762-763 in section 23). Yet, as Scholem notes, the term *Maaseh Merkabah* seems in other usages to refer to an entire type of text or set of rituals and not only to the two specific manuscripts he edited.

9. The date of *Maaseh Merkabah* is discussed in Chapter 2, pages 00-00.

10. In particular, Scholem built his argument around a short hymn that Rabbi Isaac Nahpa reports was said by the beasts pulling the ark (b. A.Z. 24b). Describing this hymn, Scholem states "the choice of words, the majesty of phrase and the lyrical rhythm are strongly reminiscent of the Hekhaloth hymns" (1965a, 25).

11. Scholem's heirs by and large have centered on minimalists readings of Scholem's maximalist arguments. For example, Schaefer (1984a) rejected Scholem's comparison of Paul's ascent in II Corinthians with the story of four rabbis trip to "paradise" found in the Talmud (1965a, 14-19). Schaefer's main points were that Paul's experience was auditory as opposed to the visual experiences described in the Hekhalot texts and that the account of the rabbis did not even concern ascent but instead was an allegory about four ways of reading the Torah. His main evidence is that two statements about one of the rabbis appear to contradict each other, pointing to the ascent motif as redactional and therefore secondary. "Either Ben Azzai died as the perfectly righteous man, for which he is praised in the verse of the psalm, or his death was a punishment for thinking that the shining marble stone was water. Together, they do not fit" (1984a, 26). It seems reasonable, however, that Ben Azzai made a mistake during his journey and that his death was still the death of a righteous man, something that becomes clearer the more one knows about Late Antique notions of ascent. Similarly, knowing not to call the heavenly marble "water" is one of the things that must be known in order to successfully ascend. None of the other attempts to explain the "Paradise" story can explain this motif. On Paul's ascent, see Tabor's recent work (1986). Halperin (1989) tried to reverse Scholem's order, stating that the exegetical stage of studying ascent passages in the Bible preceded the experiential stage. He has demonstrated only that there are seams in the rabbinic passages about ascent, not that rabbis did not believe in or practice ascent. P. Alexander (1984, 3) states that "it is arguable that Merkabah mysticism is as artificial and tendentious a construct as 'Gnosticism.'" He then explicates all the possible patterns of influence between this and other "tendentious constructs" (magic, gnosti-

cism, Merkabah mysticism), all of which are equally plausible because of the very definitional problems with which he begins. Merkabah mysticism may "reflect aliterary movement," while at the same time he states that "Mysticism appears to be related to permanent structure of the human mind" (!) (1984, 13).

12. These points are taken into consideration in the present study. See Chapter 2 and Appendix 1.

13. He does not however develop this point. The only setting mentioned for the use of a hymn is the New Year service of the ancient synagogue (1965a, 27). The relation between this service and the role of the hymn in ascent is not touched upon.

14. The Alenu that appears in *Maaseh Merkabah* differs only slightly from that of the standard liturgy.

15. However, he does not conclude from the presence of these hymns that the mystical experiences conveyed by their use is similar to those reflected in the magical papyri. On the contrary, he states that "there are magical and theurgic elements in Merkabah mysticism, but Merkabah mysticism is neither a magical nor a theurgic experience" (1980, 108-109).

16. For a partial bibliography, see Tambiah 1979.

17. "Function 1, or *purposive use* of language is characterization from the perspective of what speakers think or believe they are doing with their language as communicators using a goal-directed interpersonal medium." (Silverstein, 1984, 1).

18. "Function 2, or indexical meaning of speech, is a relationship of speech signal to its context of use that has been called either pragmatic (indexical) presupposition or pragmatic entailment. Briefly put, these relationships are as follows: pragmatic presupposition means that we must know something (we must presuppose some feature or features) about the context of a particular type; pragmatic means that once we know that a speech signal of a certain type has occurred, we automatically know certain entailed features of the speech situation" (Silverstein 1979, 1).

19. Here Jakobson mirrors the concern of other Russian formalists about verse structure and the manner in which the meanings of words are dependent on their placement within the composition. See also Tynianov 1981.

20. For other examples of the analysis of parallelism, see Sebeok 1964 and Fox 1977.

21. In other words, Akiba's words are examples of pragmatic entailment, creating their own contexts of use. See note 18.

22. As Silverstein explains, "it is the diagrammatic pragmatic supplication (in actual discourse sequence defined by the poetic structural chunks) of the principles of pseudo-equivalence set up by the poetic structure that enacts the transformation-by-[re]-definition of the situation" (1981, 9).

Chapter Two. Introduction to the Text

1. There is, for example, no equivalent to the story in *Hekhalot Rabbati* about the persecution of Jewish scholars by Roman authorities.

2. Rabbi Akiba is the only rabbi who safely returns from "paradise" in the famous story in b. Ḥag. 14a and is often depicted as an authority on heavenly secrets. In *Maaseh Merkabah*, he is a successful ascender, describing his "trip" and articulating details not found in the enigmatic talmudic story.

3. According to a story in b. Ber. 51a, Ishmael learned three pieces of information from the Prince of the Countenance, a major angelic figure who also appears in *Masseh Merkabah* (section 11). A different revelation theme is found in b. Ber. 7a, which states that Ishmael, while in the Temple, had a vision of Aktariel sitting on his divine throne. These two stories are very close thematically to *Maaseh Merkabah*. The encounter with the prince is similar to the angelic descent and the throne vision is reminiscent of the ascent vision, though in *Maaseh Merkabah* it does not take place in the Temple.

4. Rabbi Nehunya is connected to Ishmael as his teacher in a talmudic story (b. Shabbat 26b) and in *Hekhalot Rabbati* sends Ishmael off to consult with an angel in hopes of receiving information about the Roman persecution of Jewish scholars.

5. Minor themes are introduced by angelic figures in 24-25.

6. See Chapter 3, p. 43, n. 27.

7. Because Ishmael reportedly uses the prayers in sections 27-31, he is also connected with four additional sections where his name does not appear (sections 27-30).

8. In regard to *Maaseh Merkabah*, the point is that this text does not exhibit an unusually high number of variants or corruptions in relation to other Hekhalot texts. Nor does the composite nature of the text disqualify it for pragmatic analysis. The composite nature is not a perversion of the text but an inherent characteristic. Its composite structure does not negate the function of the text, both as to its "building blocks" and its larger totality. On this see further Chapter 1, p. 16, and Appendix 1.

9. If the texts come from the Late Antique period, as Scholem claimed, then the Hebrew is part of the general category post biblical or Mishnaic Hebrew (MH). Kutscher (1971) views MH as an outgrowth of biblical Hebrew and not an artificial language, in part because of the heavy usage of Late Biblical forms that the rabbis would not have known to select if they had simply created an artificial language. At present two strands of MH have been tentatively identified: MH 1, which represents the Hebrew spoken during the period of the second Temple; and MH 2, which is a scholarly construct developed after the destruction of the Temple when Hebrew was no longer spoken. This schema is not useful in analyzing *Maaseh Merkabah*. As Alexander states about the language of III Enoch,

"the exact character of its language has never been investigated" (1983, 225). A detailed study of the relation between *Maaseh Merkabah* and other Late Antique and Medieval Hebrew texts is beyond the scope of this investigation.

10. The Aramaic phrases appear in sections 11 and 13.

11. Chapter 1, p. 00. Also see the discussion of parallels in Appendix 1.

12. H. Odeberg 1973, esp. 32-38.

13. Scholem comments on *Third Enoch* in several places, including 1965, 17 n. 19, where he states that "Third Enoch already reinterprets, and, wrongly, some older Merkabah traditions that a third-century writer could not have misunderstood." Alexander has located two possible instances of such reinterpretations, which Scholem failed to make explicit (1973, 227). See also, J. Greenfield's introduction to the second edition of Odeberg's *Third Enoch* (1983, xi-xvii).

14. Alexander (1983, 225-226) rejects arguments such as the peaceful attitude of the text constituting evidence of positive interactions with Sasanian Persia in the third and fourth centuries. He also rejects a nine to tenth century date, suggested by Milik, and finally concludes, "It is impossible to reach a very firm conclusion as to the date of 3 Enoch" (1983, 228).

15. See the discussion of parallels in Appendix 1.

16. On the Hasidei Ashkenaz, see Dan 1968 and Marcus 1981.

17. Alexander's reasons for suspecting Palestinian origins include (1) the appearance of Merkabah doctrines in early Palestinian texts, (2) the attribution of the stories to Palestinian rabbis, (3) the appearance of Palestinian apocalyptic traditions in *Enoch*, and (4) references to Palestinian locations and figures in *Hekhalot Rabbati*. He states that the greater elaboration of Hekhalot ideas in Babylonia may have been due to the freer attitude of the Babylonian mystics about disclosing doctrines or simply to the greater development of the material there (1983, 232).

18. Alexander notes that *Wilon* is the Babylonian equivalent of the Palestinian term *Shamayim* (1983, 296, n. f.).

19. Alexander posits a Babylonian origin for *III Enoch* based on the close parallels to the Babylonian Talmud and the occurrence of the name *Metatron* on Babylonian magical bowls (1983, 229).

20. Among the many discussions of the power of the divine name, some of the more important ones are Zunz 1855, 145ff; Blau 1898; Bacher 1901; Marmorstein 1927; Kohler 1929; Lauterbach 1930-31; Urbach 1979, 124-134; Simon 1986, 394-431; Fossum 1985, 76-87, 241-256. Discussions of Jewish magic also include references to the transformational power of the divine Name, as for example Trachtenberg 1977.

21. See discussion and notes that follow.

22. Several scholars, for example Cohon (1951), have argued that Exodus

20:7 forbids the utterance of God's name. This is true only of the translations of the verse found in the Septuagint and the Aramaic Targums, which shows that the prohibition had developed by the time of these translations. The enigmatic "I am who I am" of Exodus 3:14-15 is also cited as evidence that God's name is secret. However, the very same verses reveal the name *Yahweh*. Kohler (1929, 50) note that Lev. 24:16 was only later interpreted as meaning any utterance of the name.

23. A variety of biblical verses refer to God's word as creative, including for example "By the word of the Lord the heavens were made" (Psalms33:6). On the suspect history of interpretation of these verses, see Appendix 2. While the power of the deity's name is a familiar theme in many religions, we are interested in a more particular theme, that the deity created the world by uttering his name.

24. Of the ten measures of magic that descended to earth, Egypt received nine (b. Kid. 49b).

25. This quote is from the Similitudes, a section of Enoch dated to the late second century B.C.E. See Charlesworth 1983, 5-12.

26. The *Book of Jubilees* dates from the second century B.C.E. See Charlesworth 1983, 43-44.

27. The Prayer of Manasseh is found in the Apostolic Constitutions and is dated ranging from the second century B.C.E. to the first century C.E. Cf. Charlesworth 1985, 625-634.

28. The Targumic evidence is beyond the scope of this study. See Janowitz 1989. Fossum (1985: 249) points to the use of the name IAW to stabilize creation in PGM XII, 539 and mentions Scholem's comparison of this text with the Valentinian uses of "IAO". For rabbinic parallels, see below.

29. Many of the discussions of the divine name mentioned in note 20 contain references to prohibitions against uttering the name. Similar themes are found in a variety of nonrabbinic sources. For example, the Community Rule forbids uttering the divine name (Cols. vi-vii). Philo says both that the deity is nameless, a common philosophical theme, and that the name should not be uttered (De vita Mos. i. 614; ii, 638). Marmorstein draws attention to Deissman's discussion of the Magic Tablet of Adrumtem (I adjure you by the sacred name which is not uttered) and the story from Atrapanus (Fragment 3b) in which Moses whispers the divine name in the ear of the pharoah, who falls down, and Moses revives him (1927, 18).

31. It would be impossible to date all of the texts we will mention, and that would still fail to supply dates for all of the stories they contain. The point of this survey is to show the types of stories told about the divine name. The particular configuration of *Maaseh Merkabah* will be examined later.

32. Sanh. 10:1, cf t. Sanh. XII, 9.

33. b. Kid. 71a also describes the characteristics desirable in a person wishing

to learn the name. B. Pes. 50a repeats the same story as b. Kid. 71a about Rav's restriction from saying the Name. It also reports that in the world to come the Name will be uttered in the same manner as it is written, an escatological unification of language.

34. On not naming (mentioning the names of) other deities, see b. Sanh. 63b on Ex. 23:13, Mek. on Ex. 23:12 and t. AZ. vi, 11, all cited by de Lange 1976, 183, n. 23.

35. On the automatic efficacy of curses, see for example, b. Ber. 56b and b. Sanh. 90b.

36. A complete analysis of the linguistic ideology of the Hebrew Scriptures is beyond the scope of this study. However, see Appendix 2.

37. This same passage also states that the curse of a sage, uttered "without cause," still takes effect.

38. Creation by means of the letter *H*, Genesis Rabba 12, 10 (Theodor). This world created by *H*, the next by *Y*, b. Men. 29b, j. Ḥag. 77c. Cf. Fossum 1985, 254, n. 30.

39. The Talmudic version does not directly state that the letters are from the divine name, though this was how the story was later understood. Cf. Blau (1898, 122); Fossum (1985, 246); and *Hekhalot Rabbati* 9.

40. These stories have been repeated to varying degrees by scholars, cf. Gruenbaum 1901; Marmorstein 1927; Cohon 1951.

41. In the past, the men of the Great Synagogue, the generation under the persecution (Hadrian's) and the generations of Hezekiah and Zedekiah knew and used the Name (See the discussion in Midrash Psalms 36.8). In the future, everyone will know the Name (b. Kid. 71a, Eccl. R. 3:11).

42. The name was given to the Israelites in the desert inscribed either on a crown or a weapon, cf. Midrash Psalms 36.8 and Midrash Numbers 12.3. Kohler [1929] connects the crown in Avot 1:13 with this crown and cites b. Megilah 28b, b. Ned. 62a, and Abd. R. Natan I. 16.

43. Marmorstein's discussion, minus his attempt to construct a unitary history of the Name, includes references to stories about the restriction of the Name to the Temple and the priests. Sometimes, even the priests are portrayed as reciting the Name in a low tone (literally, "swallowing"). He also notes the many other stories in which in the Name is used, as for example, stories in which individuals greet each other by the Name (1927, 20 ff).

44. The story also states that this situation will be reversed in the world to come.

45. Sanh. 7:5 and b. Sanh. 91a. Compare b. Sanh. 55a.

46. b. Sanh. 56a and 60a.

47. The Name also was used to enable Solomon to fly, cf. b. Sanh. 95a. A particularly interesting story about flying by means of the Name recounts how a woman used the divine Name to ascend to heaven and the deity turned her into a star. Cf. Midrash Abkir, Yalkut Simoni 44, Bereshit Rabbati (Albeck), 29, 14-31, 8, and Raymond Martin *Pugio Fidei* 1687, 937-39.

48. Buber 140a. See also Midrash Hallel; Jellinek 1937.

49. Genesis Rabba 39 sec. 14 (Theodor 378-9). Scholem (1965, 217f.) compares this story with the creation of a homocluous by Simon Magus (Ps. Clementine Homilies II, 26; Rehm p. 46) and also to later stories about the golem.

50. Song of Songs Rabba 7:9. Daniel, by kissing it, either erases or removes the Name from the statue.

51. For elaborations of the story, see Scholem 1965b, 166 ff.

52. Over eighty years ago, Gruenbaum (1901) argued that the Hebrew term came from an Aramaic equivalent found in the Targums. The root *PRS* is used, for example, in the translation of Judges 13:8, where an angel refuses to reveal his name because it is "Meforash." See Chapter 5, pp. 102-3, and Janowitz 1989.

Chapter Three. Translation and Notes

1. For descriptions of the manuscripts and further documentation, see Appendix One.

2. There are a few exceptions to this, such as the emendation in line 1048, where 0 1531 is followed. The other manuscripts are very close to 0 1531 and the hail image is common in Hekhalot texts.

Chapter Four. The Patterns and Poetics of Ascent: Employing the Name

1. The hymns are set apart from the reported-speech frames in part by their formal characteristics; that is, by the recurring use of linguistic units call attention to the hymns' structures. They are further distinguished from the frames because they follow verbs of speaking such as "I said" or "he prays" or more explicit introductions such as "this is the prayer." As to their placement in the text, they are the most deeply embedded layers, the kernels of reported speech. In many instances the first and last lines are formulaic blessing markers (Blessed are you), which signal to the reader that a new and distinct literary composition is beginning and, in turn, ending. These mini-formulas serve to demarcate the formulas and at the same time their presence signals that blessing is in action. Each opening and closing is an epitome of the blessing process, summing up the action carried

out by the recitation of the entire formula. They state that the deity is blessed and at the same time "bless" him. See also Mowley 1965; Murtonen 1959; and Heinemann 1977.

2. See discussion pp. 47-56.

3. This does not mean that the Name will not be interpreted as having some distinct meaning, as for example connecting the name *YHWH* with the root *to be.* Cf. p. 48 n. 22.

4. Hymns are found in section 1, 4, 5, 6, 9, 15, 16, 25, 27-33.

5. Examples include 32:1054-56, 1057-58, and 31:974-979.

6. The exact citation from Isaiah 6:3 is found in 5:187, 16:605, 32:1050, and 33:1121. These citations incorporate the heavenly model most directly into the text.

7. We will return to the issue of sound symbolism later.

8. Extended noun phrases include thousands of thousands of thousands/myraids of myraids of myraids (4:125-126); king of kings of kings (5:160, 15:542) and eternities of eternities of eternities (30:963). The widespread use of noun constructs is basic to Hebrew, a language weak in adjectives and adverbs. Noun constructs are used for the superlative, the "most kingly-king." These constructs, when they repeat the same word, add to the density of the text.

9. Here the noun construct has been extended beyond the sense limit; while the king of kings is clear as to its meaning, another "king" creates a more complex hierarchy but cannot logically extend the king-over-kings image. As with the expanding, gigantic numbers, the relation between elements is more important than the "meaning" when dealing with infinite or "cosmic" kingness.

10. This is even more vivid in the Hebrew, due to the lack of a finite present tense form of the verb *to be.* The rotating phrases are built up of a string of images similar to the strings of single words. Here each "word" is a double recitation of the same word, combining linear progression and duality. The use of the preposition *in* also adds a nesting effect, contributing a new layering to the text. Similar reversible phrases occur in section 8.

11. *His song* i.e., praise of the deity, consists of the repetition of the words and the sounds of the words *his song.*

12. This device is found in almost every hymn; as for example, "Your name is great and mighty in all might" (4:97).

13. Silverstein explains, "Just such a definitional form is the perfect vehicle for metaphorical pseudo-definition, where we are not dealing with metasemantic equivalence of conceptual categories" (1981, 4).

14. As noted earlier, charges of blasphemy include the use of attributes. The Name is so powerful that even Name substitutes have derived power.

15. It is this quality that Scholem was striving to capture when he stated that the Name was the metaphysical origin of all languages (1972, 63). The term *metaphysical*, however, fails to include the "magical" aspects of the name.

16. The words that are repeated include *throne, chambers, holy, name, earth, heaven, bless, praise, fire, generations, now, kingdom, might, great, justice, eternal, wisdom, king, world.* One example of the layering is "You stretched out the heavens, you established your throne, and the great name is adorned on the throne of your glory. You laid out the earth, you established in it a throne as a footstool for your feet" (lines 92-95).

The throne is first juxtaposed with the upper realm. God's name also is connected with the realm and with the throne. The word *throne* is then repeated, but this time in relation to the creation of the lower world. Earth also has its throne. This throne is still called a throne but is now, in terms of position, a footstool for the deity. The layering of the worlds is not only described but actually copied in the structure of these lines. Each layer has some of the same elements but, as always, assumes its position in the hierarchy. What to us may be a throne is only a footstool when compared to the more kingly king's throne.

17. Direct repetition of an entire phrase occurs with "Adonai is God" (5:166) and "Blessed is your Name alone (27:859-60, 65)." Both of these occur directly before the densest lines of the hymns.

18. A short syntactical pattern (verb + preposition + noun) may be repeated several times (eight times, 15:44-52) in one instance; whereas, in another syntactic pattern, phrases may be expanded or contracted from line to line.

19. God spoke sound and not sense because his Name, as described earlier, has primarily reference and not "sense".

20. Reported speech, like indirect speech, must be characterized not only by the reported utterance but also by the predicate frame chosen by the reporter to introduce the utterance, ranging from a simple "X said" to "X inquired of Y . . .?" This mode of transmission contains a built-in analysis or dissection of the utterance, the choice of reported verb to frame the speech event. The verbs and other words chosen as frames exhibit the manner in which the author of the frame, not the primary speaker, viewed the utterance. As Voloshinov writes, "Reported speech is speech within speech, message within message, and at the same time also speech about speech, message about message" (1978, 149).

21. Voloshinov explains, "once it becomes a constructional unit in the author's speech, into which it has entered on its own, the reported message concurrently becomes a theme of that speech. It enters into the latter's thematic design precisely as reported, a message with its own autonomous theme; the autonomous theme thus becomes a theme of a theme" (1978, 149).

22. For a more detailed discussion of the frames, see the end of Appendix 1. The exact same frame is never used twice in a row. The frames, however, have a strong general similarity. All the participants seem to take part in the same dialogue, lending a sense of continuity to the distinct sections.

23. Compare Searle's sincerity conditions (1969, 60-68).

24. One of the angels tells Ishmael that the mystery is not his private property but belongs to each person who recites the prayer. The frames signal this most dramatically in section 4, where the form suddenly breaks and Ishmael states. "hence listen to what R. Akiba said to me and revealed to me in order that every person who has in his heart..." Previously, the reader's presence was implied in each instance of "Ishmael said." Here, the presence of the implied reader is made more explicit, as Ishmael leans out of the frame and signals directly to the reader to listen to him. We encounter a problem at this point, however, because the New York manuscript has an unclear reading for this line and this argument must be based on the other manuscripts.

25. There is no difference between remembering the remembering of the Name, remembering the Name, and using the Name. Compare the attempt to distinguish "use" and "mention," Lyons (1971, 5-10).

26. Notice that the framing devices, being both sequential and box within a box, have the force of an indexical icon of the construction of the heavens; in the highest dwells the deity whose words/names are the innermost layer of quoted speech. The "ascent" through multiple framings linguistically is in fact ritually ascending to the status of dweller in the uppermost heaven.

27. See Appendix 1.

Chapter Five. The Pragmatics of Ascent and the Problem of Ritual Language

1. Sacrifices, for example, appear to have been silent; the only formula for a sacrifice if the first-fruits offering in Deut. 26:5.

2. See Chapter 3, note 20.

3. On the Torah as a collection of names, see Scholem 1965b and Idel 1981.

4. *Targum Neofiti* is replete with these interpretations. The debate unfortunately has been cast in terms of "hypostization" or attempts to avoid anthropomorphism. This is despite the lack of precision of the former term and the contradiction of the latter term by the simultaneous anthropomorphic descriptions of the deity. See Janowitz, 1988.

5. This is why Austin began with explicit primary performatives (I promise). See Silverstein 1979.

6. PRE 12, 11 and Tanhumna (Buber) Yitro 14.

7. Gruenwald 1969; 360; Num.R.10, 1 and ExR. 29, 9.

8. Tabor outlines ten elements that are "paradigmatic of the model as a whole" (1986, 87). These include (1) a mortal is taken up to the highest heaven;

(2) the ascent is an extraordinary privilege; (3) the way is fraught with danger and can only be successfully undertaken through divine permission and power; (4) there is a great distance between the earthly and heavenly realms with increasing beauty and splendor (or danger for the uninvited) as one moves up and an increasing sense of alienation from the world below; (5) the ascent itself is a transforming experience in which the candidate is progressively glorified; (6) the climax of the journey is an encounter with the highest god; (7) one is given secret revelations or shown mysteries; (8) the ascent is followed by a return to the world below to live on as a mortal; (9) what is seen and heard can be selectively passed on to those who are worthy; and (10) the one who has ascended faces the opposition of lower spiritual power upon his return. All of these elements are found in *Maaseh Merkabah*.

9. Hoffman belongs to this group of scholars when he describes rabbinic liturgy as having "no semantic meaning whatsoever" (1981, 121).

Appendix One. The Textured Evidence

1. Schaefer 1981, viii-x. The manuscripts also are briefly described in his 1977 article.

2. See also P. Alexander's cautionary comments about a critical edition, 1983, 224-25.

3. Scholem's edition 4/Schaefer's edition, paragraphs 547-49, 5/550-51, 6/554-55, 11/560-62, 15/566-68, 23/581-82, 24/583-84, 32/592-94, 33/595-96.

4. See Table 1.

5. M 22 lacks the final phrase of N 8128 *and gives him permission to catch sight and he is not damaged.* The "..." appears after "to me."

6. The form of first listing a set of objects (fig leaf, olive oil, and silver cup, etc.) and then expounding on each one also is not found elsewhere in the text.

7. *Maaseh Merkabah* cites the heavenly chorus of from Isaiah 6:3 and the river of fire from Daniel 7:10. In addition, the imagery of the heavenly realm derives from the visions of Ezekiel, see also Alexander's brief discussion of Old Testament citations in III Enoch (1983, 229).

8. These two sections deal with the number of winds from the wings of the cherubim and the number of chariots. Both of them are exegetical, citing a biblical passage for each wind or chariot described. Thus, in spite of their similar introductory question, the bulk of each section is very different from the material found in *Maaseh Merkabah*. Again, this contrasts the exegetical and narrative nature of *III Enoch* with the ritual concerns of *Maaseh Merkabah*.

9. The formulas in sections 11 and 13 are not included in the hymnic analysis because of these difficulties. They are not sufficiently long to study the poetic devices, as for example in section 13 where they are only letter clusters. They lack the parallelistic compositions of the other formulas as well.

10. No angel initiates dialogue in the Akiban sections.

11. The issue of Aramaic has already been discussed.

12. The enumerations, which also exhibit extensive patterning, are studied along with the formulas in Chapter 4 (sections 3, 6, 9, and 10).

13. For other examples of this problem, see lines 1038-49 and 1112-20.

14. Some images are obscured by the appearance of a single corrupt word (lines 1049, 189, 139) while others may be "meaningful" but still unclear (why the term *excommunicate* in line 308?)

15. See, for example, lines 534, 561 and 887-88.

Bibliography

Alexander, P. 1983. "3 (Hebrew Apocalypse of) Enoch". In *The Old Testament Pseudepigraphia*, edited by J. Charlesworth, pp. 223-315. New York: Doubleday.

——. 1984. "Comparing Merkabah Mysticism and Gnosticism: An Essay in Methodology." *Journal for Jewish Studies* 35, 1:1-17.

Austin, J. L. 1962. *How to Do Things with Words*. Cambridge, Mass.: Harvard University Press.

Bacher, W. 1901. "Shem ha-Meforash." In *Jewish Encyclopedia*, vol. 11:262-264.

Barr, James. 1961. *The Semantics of Biblical Language*. Oxford: Oxford University Press.

Blau, Ludwig, 1898. *Das atljüdische Zauberwesen*. Leipzig.

——. 1901. "Sandalfon." *Jewish Encyclopedia*, vol. 11:30-40.

Bloch, Maureice, 1893. "Die Yordei Merkavah, die Mystiker der Gaonenzeit und ihr Einfluss auf die Liturgie." *Monatschrift für Gechichte und Wissenchaft des Judentums*. 37:18-25, 69-74, 256-266, 305-311.

Bloch, Maurice, 1974. "Symbols, Song, Dance and Features of Articulation: Is Religion an Extreme Form of Traditional Authority?" *European Journal of Sociology* 15:55-81.

Charlesworth, James. 1983-5. *The Old Testament Pseudepigrapha*. New York: Doubleday. Vols 1-11.

Cohon, Samuel. 1951. "The Names of God. A Study in Rabbinic Theology." *Hebrew Union College Annual*, 579-604.

Dan, Joseph. 1968. *The Secret Torah of the German Pietists*. Jerusalem: Masad Bialik. (Hebrew)

De lange, Nicolas. 1976. *Origen and the Jew. Studies in Jewish-Christian Relations in Third Century Palestine.* Cambridge: Cambridge University Press.

Dornseiff, F. 1925. *Das Alphabet in Mystik and Magie.* 2d ed. Leipzig.

Fossum, Jarl. 1985. *The Name of God and the Angel of the Lord.* Tübingen, Germany: J. C. B. Mohr.

Fox, James. 1977. "Roman Jakobson and the Comparative Study of Parallelism." In *Roman Jakobson: Echoes of His Scholarship,* edited by D. Armstrong and C. H. van Schooneveld, pp. 59-90. Lisee, Netherlands: Peter de Ridder.

Grether, Oskar. 1934. *Name und Wort Gottes im Alten Testament.* Giessen, Germany: Toepelman.

Gruenbaum, M. 1901. *Gesammelte Aufsatze zur Sprach-und Sagenkunde.* Berlin: Calvary.

Gruenwald, Ithamar 1969. "New Passages from the Hekhalot Literature." *Tarbis* 38:354-72.

———. 1980. *Apocalyptic and Merkabah Mysticism.* Leiden, Netherlands: Brill.

Halperin, David. 1980. *The Merkabah in Rabbinic Literature.* New Haven, Conn.: American Oriental Society.

———. 1981. "Origen, Ezekiel and Merkabah Mysticism." *Church History* 50 3:261-75.

Hawyard, R. 1977-78. "The Holy Name of the God of Moses and the Prologue of St. John's Gospel." *New Testamente Studies* 25:16-32.

———. 1981. *Divine Name and Presence: The Memra.* Totowa, N. J.: Allanheld, Osmun.

Heinemann, Joseph. 1977. *Prayer in the Talmud.* Berlin: De Gruyter.

Hoffman, Lawrence, 1981. "Censoring in and Censoring out: A Function of Liturgical Language." In *Ancient Synagoges,* edited by Joseph Gutman, pp. 19-37. Chico, Calif.: Scholars Press.

Idel, Mosche, 1981. "Perceptions of the Torah in the Hechalot Literature and Its Development in Kabbalah." *Jerusalem Studies in Jewish Thought*: 23-84 (Hebrew).

Jakobson, Roman. 1960. "Linguistics and Poetics." In *Style in Language,* edited by T. Sebeck, pp. 350-73, Cambridge, Mass.: MIT Press.

———. 1966. "Grammatical Parallelism and Its Russian Facet." *Language.* 42:399-429.

———. 1972a. "On Linguistic Aspects of Translation." In *Selected Writings,* vol. 5:155-75. The Hague, Holland: Mouton.

———. 1972b. "The Dominent." In *Readings in Russian Poetics: Formalist and Struc-*

turalist Views, L. Matejka and K. Pomorska, pp. 82-87, edited by Ann Arbor: University of Michigan Press.

Jakobson. Roman, and L. Waugh. 1979. *The Sound Shape of Language.* Bloomington: Indiana University Press.

Janowitz, Naomi. 1984. "Parallelism and Framing Devices in a Late Antique Ascent Text." In *Semiotic Mediation* edited by E. Mertz and R. Parmentier, pp. 155-175. New York: Academic Press.

——. 1989. "Re-creating Creation: The Metapragmatics of Divine Speech." In *Reflexive Language: Reported Speech and Metapragmatics* edited by J. Lucy. Cambridge: Cambridge University Press.

Jellinek, Adolph. 1937. *Bet Ha-Midrash*, 6 volumes, Jerusalem: Bamberger and Wahrmann.

Keenan, Elinor. 1975. "A Sliding Sense of Obligatoriness: The Polystructure of Malagasy Oratory." In *Political Language and Oratory in Traditional Society*, M. Bloch, edited by New York: Academic Press.

Kohler, Kaufman. 1929. *The Origins of the Church and Synagogue.* New York: Macmillan.

Kutscher, E. 1971. "Mishnaic Hebrew." *Encyclopedia Judaica*, vol. 16:1590-1607.

Lyons, John. 1971. "Naming." In *Semantics*, Vol. 1, Section 7.5: 215-33. Cambridge: Cambridge University Press.

Marcus, Ivan. 1981. *Piety and Society: The Jewish Poetists of Medieval Germany.* Leiden, Netherlands: Brill.

Marmorstein, A. 1927. *The Old Rabbinic Doctrine of God.* Jews' College Publication no.10. London: Oxford University Press.

McNamara, Martin. 1966. *The New Testament and the Palestinian Targum of the Pentateuch.* Rome: Pontifical Biblical Institue.

Moore, Sally Falk, and Barbara Myerhoff, eds. 1977. *Secular Ritual.* Assen, Netherlands: Von Gorum.

Mowley, H. 1965. "The Concept and Content of Blessing in the Old Testament." *The Bible Translator* 19:74-80.

Murtonen, A. 1959. "The Use and Meaning of the Words *lebarek* and *berakah* in the Old Testament." *Vetus Testamentum* 9:158-77.

Odeberg, Hugh. 1973 1928. *Third Enoch.* 2d ed. New York: Ktav. 1st ed. 1928, Cambridge: Cambridge University Press.

Procksch, O. 1967. "The Word of God in the Old Testament." In *Theological Dictionary of the New Testament*, edited by G. Kittel, vol. 4:91-100. Grand Rapids, Mich.: Erdsman.

Quispel, G. 1955. "The Gospel of Truth." In *Jung Codex*, edited by H. C. Puech,

G. Quispel, and W.C. van Unnik, pp. 68-78. London: Mowbray, New York: Morehouse-Gorham Co.

Sapir, Edward. 1925. "Sound Patterns in Language." *Language* vol. 1:37-49.

Schaefer, Peter. 1977. "Prolegamena zu einer kritischer Edition und Analyse der Merkava Rabba." *Frankfurter Judaistische Bietraege* 5:65-83.

———. 1981. *Synopse zur Hekhalot-Literatur.* Tübingen, Germany: J. C. B. Mohr.

———. 1984a. "New Testament and Hekhalot Literature: The Journey into Heaven in Paul and in Merkabah Mysticism." *Journal of Jewish Studies* 35, no. 1:17-35.

———. 1984b. "Review of Gruenwald, Chernus, and Halperin." *Journal of the American Oriental Society* 104, no. 3:357-41.

———. 1984c. "Tradition and Redaction in Hekhalot Literature." *Journal for the Study of Judaism* 14, no. 2:172-81.

Scholem, Gershon. 1941. *Major Trends in Jewish Mysticism.* New York: Schocken.

———. 1965a. *Jewish Gnosticism, Merkabah Mysticism and Talmudic Tradition.* New York: Jewish Theological Seminary of America.

———. 1965b. *On the Kabbalah and Its Symbolism.* New York. Schocken.

———. 1972. "The Name of God and the Linguistic Theory of the Kabbala" *Diogenes* 79:59-80; 80:164-94.

Schwab, Moses. 1897. "Vocabulaire de l'angelogie." In *Memories divers savants Academie des Incriptions*, pp. 113-430, Ser. 1, 102.

Searle, John. 1969. *Speech Acts: An Essay in the Philosophy of Language.* Cambridge: Cambridge University Press.

———. 1971. "The Problem of Proper Names." In *Semantics*, edited by D. Steinberg and L. Jakobovits, pp. 134-141. Cambridge: Cambridge University Press.

Sebeok, T.A. 1964. "The Structure and Content of Cheremis Charms." In *Language in Culture and Society*, edited by D. Hymes and James Fox, pp. 356-71. New York: Harper and Row.

Segal, Alan. 1980. "Heavenly Ascent in Hellenistic Judaism, Early Christianity and Their Environment." In *Aufstieg und Niedergang der Roemische Welt*, edited by Wolfgang Haase, Principat II, 23:1333-94. Berlin: Walter de Gruyter.

Selingsohn, Max. 1901. "Nehunya ben Hakana." *Jewish Encyclopedia*, vol. 9:212-13.

Silverstein, Michael. 1976. "Shifters, Linguistic Categories and Cultural

Descriptions." In *Meaning in Anthropology*, edited by K. Basso and H. Selby, pp. 11-55. Albuquerque: University of New Mexico.

———. 1978. "Language Structure and Linguistics Ideology." In *The Elements*, edited by P. Clyne, W. Hanks, and C. Hofhauer pp. 193-247. Chicago: Chicago Linguistic Society, Paris Section.

———. 1981. "Metaforces of Power in Traditional Oratory." Unpublished Lecture.

———. 1984. "Culture of Language in Chinookan Narrative Texts; or, On Saying That . . . in Chinook." In *Grammar Inside and Outside the Clause* edited by J. N. Nichols and A. Woodbury. Cambridge: Cambridge University Press.

Simon, Marcel. 1986. *Verus Israel.* English translation. Oxford: Oxford University Press.

Smith, Morton, 1963. "Observations on Hekhalot Rabbati." In *Biblical and Other Studies*, edited by A. Altmann, pp. 142-60. Cambridge, Mass.: Harvard University Press.

Tabor, James. 1986. *Things Unutterable: Paul's Ascent to Paradise in its Greco-Roman, Judaic, and Early Christian Contexts.* Lanham Md.: University Press of America.

Tambiah, S. J. 1979. "A Performative Approach to Ritual." *Proceedings of the British Academy*: 113-69.

Thiselton, A. C. 1974. "The Supposed Power of Words in the Biblical Writings." *Journal of Theological Studies* 5:283-99.

Trachtenberg, J. 1977. *Jewish Magic and Superstition.* New York: Atheneum.

Tynianov, Yuri. 1981. *The Problem of Verse Language.* Ann Arbor Mich.: Ardis.

Urbach, Ephraim. 1979. *The Sages.* Jerusalem: Magnes Press.

Vermes, Geza. 1960-61. "The Targumic Versions of Genesis 4:3-16." *Annual of the Leeds Oriental Society* 3:81-114.

Voloshinov, V. N. 1978. "Reported Speech." In *Readings in Russian Poetics: Formalist and Structuralist Views*, edited by L. Matejka and K. Pomorska, pp. 149-75. Ann Arbor: University of Michigan Press.

Von Rad, Gerhard. 1965. *Old Testament Theology.* Edinburgh: Oliver and Boyd.

Wheelock, Wade. 1982. The Problem of Ritual Language. *Journal of the American Academy of Religion* 50:49-71.

Zunz, Leopold. 1855. *Die Synagogale Poesie des Mittelalters.* Berlin: Springer.

Index